Contents

DANCE INSTRUCTION

Science Applied to the Art of Movement

Judith A. Gray, PhD

Human Kinetics Books
Champaign, Illinois

To my sons, Andrew and Jonathan, to Allan,
and to my students over the years,
from whom I learned the art of teaching.

Library of Congress Cataloging-in-Publication Data

Gray, Judith Anne, 1939-
    Dance instruction : science applied to the art of movement /
Judith A. Gray.
    p.   cm.
    Bibliography: p.
    Includes index.
    ISBN 0-87322-233-4
    1. Dancing–Study and teaching.   I. Title.
GV1589.G73   1989
792.8–dc20   89-31489
                                                      CIP

ISBN: 0-87322-233-4

Developmental Editor: Marie Roy
Copyeditor: Julie Anderson
Assistant Editor: Valerie Hall
Proofreader: Phaedra Hise
Production Director: Ernie Noa
Typesetter: Cindy Pritchard
Text Design: Keith Blomberg
Text Layout: Tara Welsch
Cover Image: Edward Pope and Judith Gray
Illustrations: Tim Offenstein
Printer: Braun-Brumfield, Inc.

Printed in the United States of America

10 9 8 7 6 5 4 3 2 1

Human Kinetics Books
A Division of Human Kinetics Publishers, Inc.
Box 5076, Champaign, IL 61825-5076
1-800-DIAL-HKP
1-800-334-3665 (in Illinois)

Foreword

I first knew Judith Gray by reputation because she was a rarity in the dance world: a person deeply invested in research, constantly probing for new scientific ideas to apply to this predominantly nonverbal arts field.

When I met Judith she was, true to form, giving a lecture on using computers with dance. I also remember our stimulating exchange during a workshop on computers and dance. I have long been interested in the direction of Judith's work, so it was with delight that I read the galley proofs to *Dance Instruction: Science Applied to the Art of Movement.*

This book is a wonderful addition to dance education. So much of what we do as dancers is felt, sensed, intuited, or remembered from former teachers. Judith brings us to a place where we can begin to validate the study of dance to persons in other disciplines and, perhaps even more importantly, where we can profit from recent advances in the sciences. To me, Judith is a self-contained exploratory network. Her skill is to take the broad areas of education, science, and technology that relate to dance, then to select and synthesize research data and present it in a clear, understandable form. I very much like her special inclusions, such as the key terms in each chapter and the simplified lists of systems that help us to retain the information she has gathered.

In this book we are invited to embrace many new ideas. We are offered an overview of a conceptual research framework. Various instructional modes are suggested. There are specific structures for observational techniques. Judith raises important questions about supervision of dance teachers, noting that dance has never had guidelines, texts, or publications that address supervision of dance teachers in the schools. I found the chapter on curriculum particularly helpful. Cogent excerpts from the writings of Elliot Eisner, the American Alliance for Art Education, and the National Dance Association plus samples of state dance curriculum guidelines give the reader an excellent grasp of this key subject. Judith is not afraid of bringing up issues like sexual politics or holographic dance in the future. I like the broadness of her thinking. She leaves the reader to expand on the concepts presented in each chapter. There are excellent ideas for student assignments and for further development by reading and writing.

I feel dance suffers from a lack of scientific study. My hope is that this book will push us into a new era of serious investigation, that it will be a catalytic agent for the dancer to become more involved in "what's out there." With each chapter we are given an overview of resources and suggested applications. We are also given a peek into the world of the future.

Thank you, Judith Gray, for motivating us to think and ponder, for giving us new tools for exploration and discovery that will help move us into the 21st century. Your gift to the dance world has long been needed.

Shirley Russon Ririe
Salt Lake City, UT

Preface

During this century the field of dance education, or "educating through dance," has spread in so many directions that, in the literature at least, no frame of reference or central forum seems to exist. Dance educators themselves range from aerobics instructors to professors of graduate dance theory courses, from child care providers to choreographers. They all seek affirmation and information; however, they have little or no access to the findings of dance education researchers. Important research articles are published in a wide variety of periodicals, often under such seemingly incongruous subject headings as architecture, computer science, sociology, physical education, anthropology, history, and philosophy. With so much descriptive and quantitative dance research being generated and disseminated, it seems timely, if not critical, to synthesize this information for all those who educate and are educated through dance. Hence this theoretical dance education resource book.

Dance Instruction describes what the dance education field is all about. The book brings together the many facets of the dance teaching/learning process while contributing to the literature in dance research. As its creator and author, I feel honored to serve my profession in this particular way because the pen, I believe, is mightier than the performance, especially when wielded by an educator. I have danced and taught dance since I was seven, when I began staging the annual neighborhood concert in my family's backyard. After many years of teaching dance in high schools, elementary schools, and kindergartens I earned my doctorate in education administration and dance education. While teaching at the University of Wisconsin-Madison in the early 1980s I began researching and writing and have published articles on dance teaching, dance technology, and dance history. From this diverse background I have drawn the theories and ideas found in this book. Although other books address the teaching methods and materials of dance, this work is unique because it includes a far greater range of topics and logically combines traditional perspectives of dance education with the latest in technology and educational research.

The book spans time from the cave drawings of a primitive dance ritual to computerized robot choreography. The book covers a myriad of subjects important to dance—from teaching and learning strategies to pastoral care support systems. A glimpse of the future of dance and dance education is provided along with an assurance that dance education is alive and well and promises to play a yet more significant role in the era of information technology when, it is predicted, the arts will come into their own. Indeed, the very existence of our field depends upon our relationship with the new technologies, and we must accept the new ways of thinking about and processing what we know about our art and communication. This book can therefore be regarded as an information source document, an interactive vehicle for the understanding and transmission of knowledge and ideas about the teaching and learning of dance.

This book can be used

- by teachers of dance education courses as a textbook;
- by dance program developers, dance curriculum designers, and dance course creators as a handbook;
- by dance administrators for dance program advocacy, review, and evaluation;
- by dance researchers as a source of avenues for further investigation;
- by dance students in all areas for study, reference, ideas, and information;
- by performers and choreographers for information on support systems, career options, and dance technology; and
- by teachers of all kinds of dance as a theoretical resource, with ample references, latest research, and professional development ideas.

The book is organized into self-contained chapters, each addressing an important aspect of the dance education field. For reference and research purposes, each chapter includes a list of key words with definitions plus suggestions for further reading. Student assignments and exercises especially designed to verify, apply, and expand the concepts in each chapter are also included. This book seeks to generate further investigation in the forms of surveys, research projects, appraisals, and qualitative studies. I hope readers will not only be edified and informed by the content but will feel encouraged to develop and strengthen the dance education field through their own professional growth activities.

This book is the first synthesis of its kind and signals the coming of age of dance education as a verifiable and vital academic discipline. I project that dance teachers will welcome this formalized, theoretically-based rationale for their instructional programs and that it will be a critical source of information for students in dance and dance education. This book provides information for performers and choreographers as well as data and substantiation for dance administrators who are promoting and strengthening their dance programs and ventures. I am pleased to submit this work to my colleagues and their students for their education and enrichment.

Acknowledgments

Very special thanks to Marie Roy for her patience and expertise, to my colleagues who shared their experience and research, to my sons Andrew and Jonathan for their loving support, and to Allan for keeping me on task.

Chapter 1
Introduction

Dance teaching is a special kind of teaching, which can neither be reduced to another form nor generalized to include other teaching fields. Because the critical issue is discerning which features of dance teaching are central to the dance learning process, and vice versa, it is more important to study the actual processes of dance teaching and learning rather than their respective merits and contents. Dance education researchers often apply the methodologies and underlying rationalities of other disciplines to their work, which is unfortunate as this can lead to assumptions that may hinder development of a strong, distinctive body of dance education knowledge.

The development, through dance education research, of a definitive area of scholarly expertise will bring unique teaching and learning processes for dance. While dance is generally accepted as a socio-cultural activity that communicates experiences in a way matched by no other media, dance education, or "education through dance," has not yet attained distinctiveness in this culture. In most pedagogical settings, dance education has not striven to be singular, to be mode specific. The relationship between the teaching process and the content of the presentation can be so distant that these elements are at odds with one another. Marshall McLuen, in *Understanding Media* (McLuen, 1964), said that the medium is the message; in dance we interpret this to mean that the body is the medium and movement is the message. In dance education, the phrase is interpreted to mean that the teaching process is the medium and what is taught is the message. If methodologies and attitudes used in dance teaching are borrowed from other disciplines, questionable consequences for the learners will result. The content of dance—the message—will lose its connection with presentation—the medium—and learners will receive a mixed stimulus or a garbled message, like being asked to drink tea from a dinner plate or to create flowing shapes while standing rigidly in rows.

Because schools, colleges, and universities in this country have offered dance instruction for little more than 50 years, teaching and learning processes are, not surprisingly, still evolving. Dance educators are currently pushing to move out from underneath the physical education umbrella toward a more independent status, though not necessarily an "art" one. The question now arises, What is the best way to teach technical proficiency, artistic creativity, or cultural sensitivity in dance? What are the appropriate modes for teaching this art? Does the mathematics teacher utilize different teaching modes for algebra, geometry, and calculus? If the medium is truly the message, then the nature of the content must determine the nature of the teaching process, which will in turn directly influence the learning process. It follows that the teaching and learning of dance rest on the immutable belief in the importance of dance in our lives. The famous dance educator Margaret H'Doubler (1978; see Figure 1.1) believes that dance can play an important part in the enrichment of an individual life—that movement is the source of meaning as well as the medium for expressing and communicating.

This chapter looks at the teaching and learning of dance from a historical perspective and defines terminology used in this book; chapter 2 presents a conceptual framework for the teaching and learning of dance. These two chapters serve as foundations for the chapters that follow.

This book has been designed to stimulate further reading, investigation, and speculation. Consequently, key terms, student activities and assignments, and recommendations for further reading are included at the end of each chapter. A bibliography follows the final chapter.

Evolution of Dance Teaching

Dance ethnologists, art historians, and anthropologists have long recognized that the performance of dance movements is as old as history itself. Paleolithic

Figure 1.1. Margaret H'Doubler.

cave drawings near Palermo in Sicily depict human figures performing what appears to be ritualistic dance (see also Figure 1.2), an observation that implies dance must have been taught and learned. Dance, together with oratory, music, tool-making, and carving, can be considered one of the earliest formal teaching disciplines. Since men and women first discovered that human movement possesses powerful expressive and evocative qualities, they have sought to retain, refine, and transmit certain skills and patterns, most frequently in the form of dance rituals or performances.

In many cultures, one person was assigned the role of conveying dance movements, usually without embellishment or innovation. Dances usually evolved over time and changed subtly rather than dramatically, subsequently requiring facilitators, trainers, or coaches (as opposed to choreographers) for their transmittal. These teachers were known variously as shamans, witch doctors, or dancing masters, or by other titles that denoted respect and indicated rank or specialization. These people and the dancers themselves have handed down pedagogical strategies and acted as dance teachers ever since leading and following became forms of teaching and learning.

Dance teachers traditionally have taught as they themselves were taught; role modeling is still dominant in the training of dance teachers. Yet the single role modeling method is less effective and less prevalent today due to the

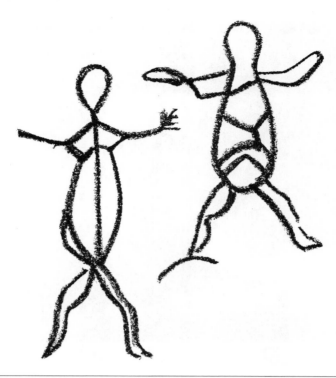

Figure 1.2.   Representation of 4,000-year-old rock paintings in Lapland. *Note.* Courtesy of J. Allan Wellman.

diversity and number of dance styles, studios, classes, and performance opportunities. Consequently, the demand for dance teachers who are trained in a variety of styles is growing. Millions of Americans are attending dance classes to study ballet, jazz, ballroom, Middle Eastern, tap, and square dancing. Dance teacher preparation is available in most states, and several states offer dance teacher certification.

The dance masters of today, whether they teach in schools, colleges, private studios, dance companies, theaters, or community facilities, determine the historical path of dance in our culture and in our lives. The teaching role is critical to the growth, sustenance, and preservation of dance in our society. This book argues that the teachers of dance, rather than the more visible performers and choreographers, drive the field of dance and shape its destiny. Behind every great dancer there is a greater teacher (see Figure 1.3). How do these teachers gain their mastery? Who is responsible for their training and educational philosophy? What do they actually teach, and how is this material organized? To whom do they pass along their knowledge, skills, and experiences? The answers to these questions effectively define the field of dance education.

Figure 1.3.   Dance teacher. *Note.* Photo courtesy of Jerry Capps.

The teaching and learning of dance exist in both horizontal and vertical historical contexts. Dance has developed breadth with styles spreading from culture to culture, while at the same time it has closely followed the chronology of history by reflecting the evolving social fabric. Dance education is sufficiently rich in concepts to comprise a salient and scholarly field of study, which can best be approached by designing a broad conceptual framework that will structure and envelop the diverse content of dance education.

Definition of Terms

Dance as used throughout this book is defined as the art of human movement, consisting of factors and conditions that are "intentionally formed and executed to evoke aesthetic feeling states" (H'Doubler, 1978, p. 16). Dance teaching is the dynamic, interactive process of transmitting skills and knowledge of dance. Further, dance teaching is the accumulative influence, appropriate or inappropriate, that a dance teacher imposes on students in an instructional (rather than a choreographic or rehearsal) situation. This definition excludes lecture or seminar situations, but may include nontraditional moving spaces.

A *dance teacher* is responsible for the preparation, presentation, and evaluation of the dance material. He or she may be formally or informally trained. A dance teacher's job is to effectively transmit the skills and knowledge of dance to learners. *Dance learner* is more difficult to define. Broadly speaking, a dance learner is anyone who participates, and registers behavioral change, in a dance instruction session. Dance learning typically requires no texts, tools, or equipment, which is also true of the study of singing, oratory, mime, improvisational theater, debating, recreation, and some physical education activities. Nonetheless, dance learning is unique. The instrument is the human body, and the materials are human movements and all that they aesthetically and technically imply. Margaret H'Doubler (1978) aptly summed this up by stating, "We are our own teacher, textbook, and laboratory" (p. 15). In order to learn dance, the student must integrate the processes of self-teaching, learning to learn, resource utilization, reflection, experimentation, and self-evaluation.

Key Terms

Dance—the art of human movement

Dance education—the teaching and learning of dance

Dance learner—one who acquires knowledge, skills, and understanding about dance

Dance pedagogy—the art and profession of teaching dance

Dance rituals—ceremonies or rites performed through dance

Dance teacher—one who provides dance instruction

Dance teaching—dance instruction

Medium—a means of communication; in dance the medium is the body

Message—that which is communicated; in dance the message is transmitted from dancer to observer

Role model—a model for others to emulate

Student Activities and Assignments

1. Research an early example of dance teaching, preferably one in a primitive society. Identify the teacher, learners, content or material, and instructional environment.
2. State the differences between:
   a. dancer and learner
   b. teacher and coach
   c. dance and dancing

d. medium and message

e. the body as instrument and the body as material

3. List the places where dance is taught in your community. What kinds of dance are taught? What subgroups of the population do these classes attract and serve? What are the qualifications of the teachers?

4. Observe a variety of teaching/learning situations. Briefly discuss the instructional methods in terms of medium and message. Evaluate each situation on a scale of 1 to 10, with 1 denoting a close relationship between the medium and the message and 10 denoting a wide disparity.

Further Reading

Dimondstein, G. (1983). Moving in the real and feeling worlds: A rationale for dance in education. *Journal of Physical Education, Recreation and Dance,* **54**(7), 42-44.

Eisner, E. (1986). The role of the arts in cognition and curriculum. *Journal of Art and Design Education,* **5**(1 & 2), 57-67.

Ellfeldt, L. (1976). *Dance from magic to art.* Dubuque, IA: W.C. Brown.

H'Doubler, M. (1966). *Dance: A creative art experience.* Madison, WI: University of Wisconsin Press.

Chapter 2
A Conceptual Framework for Research in Dance Teaching

Chapter 2 expands on the issues related to dance teaching that were raised in the introduction. This chapter describes dance teaching by means of a conceptual framework designed expressly for the understanding and investigation of dance teaching. This framework provides the scaffolding for a sound, comprehensive, and coherent instructional theory for dance. It takes into account the human and physical teaching environment, the political-administrative climate, and the outcomes for the teacher, the institution, and society. It represents the first conceptual framework designed explicitly for the empirical study of dance teaching, although its usefulness can extend to all aspects of the dance education field.

Research in dance teaching has to date been restricted to isolated studies of teacher behavior (Gray, 1983a; Lord, 1981-1982; Lunt, 1974) and limited investigations of student attitudes and achievement (Halstead, 1980; Jeffries, 1979; Oshuns, 1977). These studies were performed in the absence of a structured teaching research framework or an instructional theory of dance. The variables that these studies investigated, however, can be identified and located within the boundaries of the present framework. In this respect, they can be viewed as part of a larger, formalized context. The conclusions are thus more meaningful and more likely to lead to further dance education research. The framework that follows provides needed direction and motivation for the study of dance teaching. It should be pointed out, however, that dance teaching research has also been hindered by the absence of criteria and tools for measuring outcomes, particularly learner outcomes such as performance and achievement.

The framework is a broad-based structure containing all the probable elements and concepts related to the phenomena of dance teaching and illustrating the multiple relationships between these elements and concepts. In order to give the framework credence from a theoretical standpoint, certain criteria were established.

Description of the Framework

The framework presented in this chapter (see Figure 2.1) is a presage/process/product model similar to those designed by Mitzel (1960), Dunkin and Biddle (1974), and Harnischfeger and Wiley (1976). Within the framework the elements and concepts are sorted into three sets of variables:

1. *Presage variables*—events that occurred in the past or evolved over time
2. *Process variables*—actions and phenomena that impinge directly and contemporaneously on the teaching situation
3. *Product variables*—the resulting outcomes of the teaching process

Central to the framework is the dance teaching process itself, led by the teacher, which occurs in a moving space and which in turn is broken down into verbal, nonverbal, orientation, and mobility behaviors.

The teacher's behaviors are highly influential and critical to the material, the students, the school, and the societal outcomes. Student backgrounds and behaviors are also important, but the framework is justifiably focused directly on the teaching process itself. Figure 2.1 illustrates the presage (background)/process (dance studio)/product (outcomes) sequence. The backgrounds of the teacher and students comprise the presage component; student and teacher behaviors, the environment, the curriculum, and the climate comprise the process component; and the outcomes for teacher, students, school, and society comprise the product component.

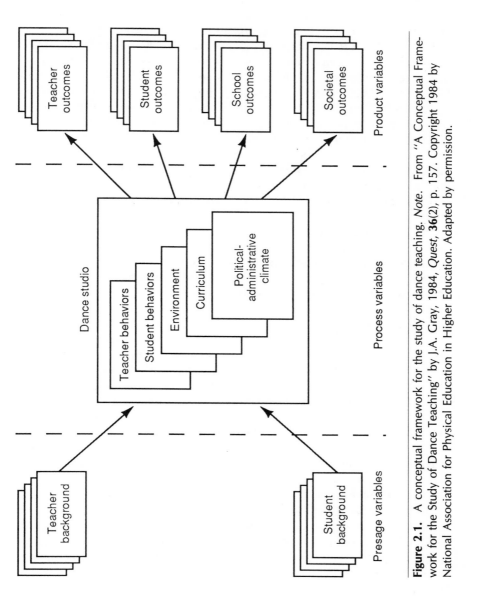

Figure 2.1. A conceptual framework for the study of dance teaching. *Note.* From "A Conceptual Framework for the Study of Dance Teaching" by J.A. Gray, 1984, *Quest, 36*(2), p. 157. Copyright 1984 by National Association for Physical Education in Higher Education. Adapted by permission.

Presage Variables

The presage component is divided into *determinants*, *experiences*, and *properties* as illustrated in Figure 2.2. Determinants are variables or elements that are established prior to teacher preparation or dance training. Dunkin and Biddle (1974) note, "Teachers, like other persons, will have been treated differently if they were born a man or a woman, if they are black or white, if they have lived in a lower-class home, if they come from a large city or a small town, if they lived in an ethnic ghetto, if they were an only child or the last child in a big family" (p. 39). The experiences of teachers and students are related to training, performance, participation, education, and overall exposure to dance. Experiences include training in dance, music, and related arts and exposure to concerts, lessons, television, recitals, and social occasions. Properties consist of measurable personality characteristics and traits, such as self-concept, creativity, and motivation. In addition, the teacher's knowledge of dance and level of dance technical skill are also considered properties. Students display a similar variety of presage properties, which are also listed in Figure 2.2. Dunkin and Biddle (1974) note that teacher properties are studied more than observable teacher determinants such as age and gender, and they speculate that the instruments for assessing such properties have a "mystique of their own" despite evidence of the influences of demographic variables on job performance in other contexts (p. 41).

Process Variables

Within the physical, social, and pedagogical arena of the dance teaching environment are a number of process concepts and elements. Figure 2.3 illustrates the four major influences that form this component.

The dance teaching *environment* consists of such physical elements as room size, teaching aids and materials, acoustics, lighting, and sound accompaniment resources. When assessing the dance teaching environment as a variable, the researcher must also consider class size and composition, amount of teaching time allotted, level of ability, and opportunities for students to learn. The *curriculum* plays an important role in the teaching process and can be evaluated in terms of objectives, organization, mission, and lesson plan structure. Dance curriculum is discussed in greater detail elsewhere in this book. The dance teaching environment is also joined with a *climate* that is pervaded by political and administrative policies and procedures such as discipline policies, fire drills, noise level limits, attendance requirements, grades, and noninstructional interruptions. Central to the process component are teacher and student *behaviors*, which can now be objectively measured and analyzed to provide the dance education field with valuable teaching/learning information. Student behaviors are typically more constrained and less exhibitory than those of the dance teacher, as students are often in a following mode. (This does not apply in creative dance or improvisation

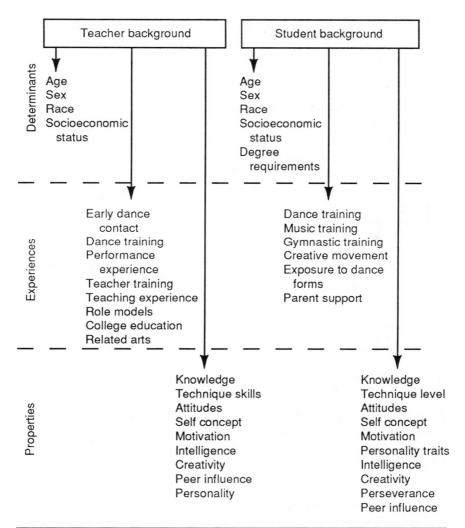

Figure 2.2.   Organization of presage variables. *Note.*   From "A Conceptual Framework for the Study of Dance Teaching" by J.A. Gray, 1984, *Quest*, **36**(2), p. 157. Copyright 1984 by National Association for Physical Education in Higher Education. Adapted by permission.

classes.) Teacher behaviors are related to the teacher's roles as information provider, guide, and monitor. All behaviors in this component are categorized as verbal, nonverbal, proxemic, and location or mobility. Research findings show the extent and influence of some of these process variables. For example, Lord (1981-1982) found that dance teachers verbalized 54 percent of the teaching time; Gray (1983a), after comparing the mobility measures

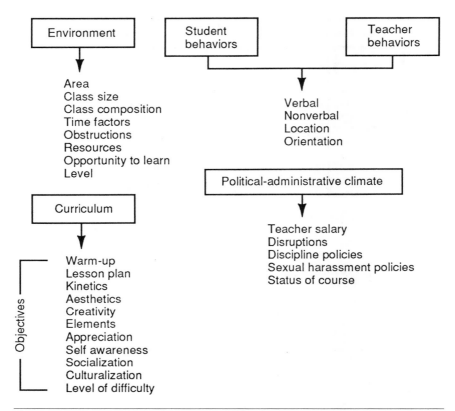

Figure 2.3. Organization of process variables. *Note.* From ''A Conceptual Framework for the Study of Dance Teaching'' by J.A. Gray, 1984, *Quest,* **36**(2), p. 158. Copyright 1984 by National Association for Physical Education in Higher Education. Adapted by permission.

of dance teachers, found that the older, more experienced teachers circulated through the teaching space more frequently and consistently than the younger, less experienced teachers.

Product Variables

The product component shown in Figure 2.4 consists of four outcome recipient groups—teachers, students, school, and community (society). Teacher outcomes include job satisfaction, self-fulfillment, professional recognition, and marketability. Student outcomes are based on personal achievement, attitude, and skill transference, and include skill mastery, level of participation, creativity, and socialization. Outcomes for school and community have both posi-

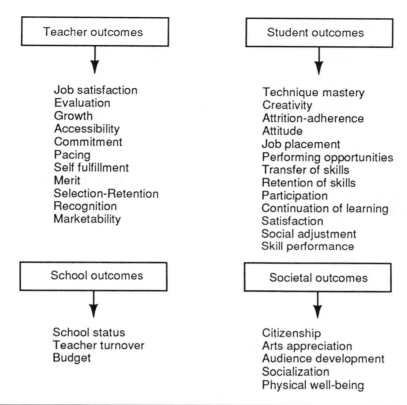

Figure 2.4. Organization of product variables. *Note.* From "A Conceptual Framework for the Study of Dance Teaching" by J.A. Gray, 1984, *Quest*, **36**(2), p. 159. Copyright 1984 by National Association for Physical Education in Higher Education. Adapted by permission.

tive and negative ramifications and are significant in that they often help determine the growth and continuance of the dance program. Concepts in this area that deserve attention are visibility, support, loyalty, funding, and values.

Justification of the Framework

The framework is substantiated through the application of six critical criteria: comprehensiveness, representativeness, integration, focus, extrapolation, and interpretation.

Comprehensiveness

Is the framework as broad and as germane as possible, including a continuum of concepts that cover prior events and experiences, present processes, and future or predictive products? Comprehensiveness ensures an evolving framework and an inherent flexibility. A theory of dance teaching develops from the acceptance or rejection of specific elements (i.e., events, experiences, processes, and products) within the aggregation of the framework.

Representativeness

Do the elements of the framework represent teaching in general and dance teaching specifically? Elements common to all teaching disciplines include student intelligence, teacher gender, and dimensions of the teaching environment. Elements specific to dance teaching include prior dance training and kinesthetic awareness. A theory of dance evolves from validating representative variables and testing the relationships between them.

Integration

Is the framework integrated on several levels? Are the elements arranged sequentially so that logical reasoning is apparent and a sense of temporal flow is created? For example, dance training typically precedes teacher training, and both precede the actual teaching of a class. Also, the concepts and their operational definitions are integrated so that theoretical constructs can emerge. An integrated framework lends itself to strong theoretical inferences and subsequent credibility.

Focus

In this framework, are the teacher's role and presence in the instructional setting focal to the analysis of the dance teaching/learning process? Any behavioral framework should clearly indicate where the focus is placed and from whom the paths of correlation radiate and converge. In any theory of dance teaching, the teacher's activities and experiences are central to the greater understanding of the pedagogical process. The effects of all other aspects of the framework are mediated through the teacher. A theory of dance teaching necessarily reflects this centrality.

Extrapolation

In order to be useful for empirical investigation, are the elements in the framework defined and arranged so they can readily be extrapolated to form predictive and causal research models? Is the framework a flexibly structured set of propositions for which data must be sought for correlational analysis?

Interpretation

After data has been gathered and analyzed, is it converted into meaningful information that is interpreted in terms of practical or theoretical significance? Interpretation is the theoretical link between the framework and further research or immediate practical application.

Uses in Research

Examining Past Research

A major strength of this framework is its amenability to prior research findings. In other words, as well as giving needed direction and ideas for future research in dance education, the structure can be used to interpret previous investigations and their results. This mapping ability, which supports a systemized theory of dance teaching, can be illustrated by examining the following research studies. Halstead (1980) compared student and teacher attitudes (presage: properties) after test subjects completed a course of creative dance (process: curriculum), and she found a positive change (product: student outcome). Oshuns (1977) found that a creative dance experience increased the self-concept (presage: property) of 7th grade students, while Jeffries (1979) determined that dance skill performance (product: student outcome) was enhanced by using preinstructional strategies (process: environment). Minton (1981) established that postural alignment (product: student outcome) improved with the use of certain verbal cues (process: teacher behavior). Thus, specific variables from the framework's systematic arrangement can be extracted for examination and investigation, a facility that lends itself to both quantitative and qualitative research.

Designing Future Research

This section demonstrates the initial formulation of a hypothesis using the conceptual framework. Using an inset of the framework (see Figure 2.5), the presage/process/product sequence is reduced to the elements that directly concern the outcome variable. For this application, the element of dance teacher accessibility will be used.

A high level of accessibility, defined as the teacher's proximity to students, represents an effective teaching strategy in a dance class. Accessibility is measured in terms of the teacher's location patterns and preferences: (e.g., the total number of cells traversed when the floor is matrixed into evenly sized cells). Background factors such as the teacher's age and gender (determinants), years of dance teaching (experience), and self-concept and motivation (properties) are thought to influence location behaviors.

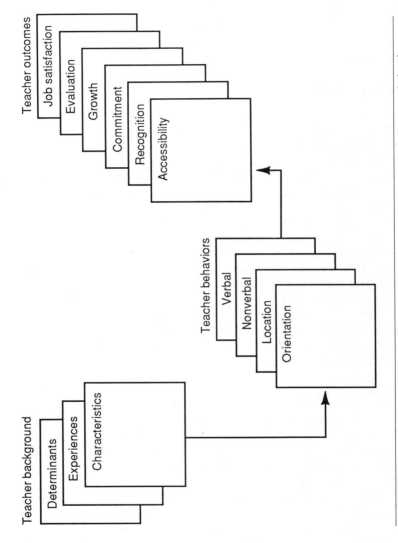

Figure 2.5. Inset from conceptual framework. *Note.* From "A Conceptual Framework for the Study of Dance Teaching" by J.A. Gray, 1984, *Quest*, **36**(2), p. 160. Copyright 1984 by National Association for Physical Education in Higher Education. Adapted by permission.

Causal Modeling

Before collecting and analyzing the data, researchers must construct a model showing variables and tentative relationships. *Causal* models are currently the most commonly used methodologies in educational research. They are characterized by data analysis techniques (such as path analysis), correlational tests for spurious relationships, estimation procedures for complex models with reciprocal linkages, and treatment of unmeasured variables (Blalock, 1964; Simon, 1957). According to Asher (1983) a causal model that not only specifies the relationship between dependent and independent variables but also includes the relationship between prior variables has greater promise of increasing our understanding of the teaching/learning process than other more rigid methodologies. For example, rather than simply hypothesizing that older and more experienced teachers are more accessible to their students, researchers might frame causally relevant questions, such as, Why might increased age and experience translate into better accessibility? Or, How do age and experience actually produce greater accessibility? Figure 2.6 shows a diagram of a causal model that indicates the effect of teacher background factors on accessibility to students.

Caveats in Using the Framework

To obtain reliable data analysis results from the investigations extrapolated from the framework, researchers must overcome three obstacles in the model-building stage.

1. The paths of the model must be well specified.
2. The key concepts must be clearly and satisfactorily defined.
3. The underlying theories must be developed and ultimately established.

"The results of one's causal analysis," warns Asher (1983), "are only as valid as the initial decisions made in building the model and operationalizing the variables" (p. 81). Causal modeling thus appears a most appropriate methodology for the study of dance teaching using the presage/process/product paradigm approach. Further, Asher (1983) maintains that "causal thinking and the construction of arrow diagrams may still make a significant contribution to theory building and hypothesis generation" (p. 81). These appear to be the critical needs in the scientific study of the dance teaching/learning process. A discussion of complex causal models within the conceptual framework must include mention of multiple indicators.

Multiple Indicators

The unknowns in dance teaching research far outweigh empirical findings, which implies the need for a data collection method that measures variables by more than one indicator. The multiple indicator approach directs the

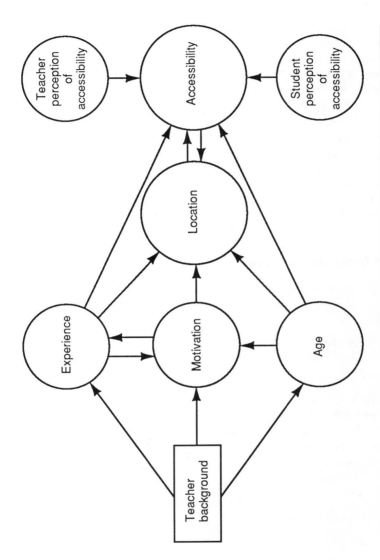

Figure 2.6. A causal model for the study of dance teacher accessibility. *Note.* From "A Conceptual Framework for the Study of Dance Teaching" by J.A. Gray, 1984, *Quest,* **36**(2), p. 161. Copyright 1984 by National Association for Physical Education in Higher Education. Adapted by permission.

researcher to find other indicators that are not necessarily equivalent. For example, accessibility can be measured by videotaping the whole class, distributing carefully designed questionnaires to students, conducting interviews with the teacher, and systematically observing the teacher's mobility patterns. The result is a multiple indicator measurement error model. Implications for comparability across settings become critical and obvious. Blalock (1982) provides a detailed discussion of this approach and is recommended for further reading.

Other Uses of the Framework

As an orderly representation of the influences and implications of dance teaching, this conceptual framework provides a foothold and also a springboard for dance researchers and practitioners. It can be used in the following ways:

1. To provide a multidimensional basis for a theoretical perspective of the dance/teaching learning process
2. To create a tangible foundation for the dance teacher training practices and programs based on tested hypotheses
3. To develop dance teacher effectiveness criteria and more effective teaching strategies
4. To encourage innovative and experimental teaching projects after tested theories of dance teaching have emerged
5. To refine dance teaching observation skills and instruments and to employ computer technology where possible
6. To inform teachers of the current state of dance teaching research

Classroom and seminar dance teachers may use this framework by applying the results of dance teaching research to their own situations or by using the structural flow of the framework as they plan and implement dance curricula and instructional formats.

Conclusions

Dance educators can improve their methods only through the guidance of an overall conceptual framework for dance education. As long as dance teaching serves to develop and preserve dance in our society, research to improve the process and the product must be rigorously pursued. It is hoped that the framework presented here will provide the structure and incentive for relevant research in dance education.

In the following chapter, the scientific approach to dance teaching focuses on the multidimensional profile of the dance teacher.

Key Terms

Accessibility—approachability

Causal—indicating or expressing an antecedent or prior event

Comprehensiveness—largeness in scope and content, encompassing the whole field of dance

Conceptual framework—an organized matrix of ideas and theories

Criteria—standards

Determinants—influencing or determining factors

Empirical research—research that relies on observation or experiments

Experiences—active participation in events or activities

Extrapolation—act of inferring or estimating by projecting information

Focus—center of interest or activity

Hypothesis—a set of facts that can be tested by further investigation

Integration—the organization of components into a harmonious whole

Interpretation—explanation or elucidation

Outcomes—natural results or consequences

Presage variables—inconstant variables that indicate future occurrence

Process variables—inconstant variables that indicate ongoing action

Properties—characteristics, traits, or attributes

Product variables—inconstant variables that indicate end results

Representativeness—quality of serving as an example of the dance field

Theory—systematically organized knowledge including assumptions, principles, and rules of procedure

Student Activities and Assignments

1. Adapt the presage/process/product paradigm to an area of the dance teaching/learning process in which you are interested. Clearly identify all the relevant variables.
2. Explain the differences in student backgrounds (presage variables) between males and females. Discuss how these differences are likely to affect the process and product variables of dance learning.
3. Using a causal model diagram, design a research study that proposes to identify the effects of environmental conditions on the teaching process. Show the paths and both the known and unknown variables.
4. Draw analogies between using the computer technology model (input/output) in data processing and using the presage/process/product model in teaching.

Further Reading

Blalock, H.M. (1964). *Causal inferences and measurement in nonexperimental research*. Chapel Hill, NC: University of North Carolina Press.
Dunkin, M.J., & Biddle, B.F. (1974). *The study of teaching*. Boston: Allyn and Bacon.

Chapter 3
Dance Teaching: Observing and Analyzing

Chapter 2 explained that a rational and scientific study of dance must be conducted within an organized matrix of ideas and concepts. Dance may be the oldest art but the study of dance is a young science. Dances have been passed on from generation to generation and from one culture to another (vertically and horizontally) by means of the teaching/learning process. By contrast, the science of observing and recording these behaviors is less than one hundred and fifty years old. Dance has always lent itself to subjective, qualitative descriptions, hence the established and well-documented field of dance criticism. Recently, the field of professional choreographic evaluation has developed for the purpose of promotion, tenure, and retention of college and university dance faculty (Carver & Frangione, 1985). This effort promises to validate and elevate artistically productive dance teachers in higher education.

Carver & Frangione (1985) report, "Dance has reached full-grown maturity in the academic setting and must accept the consequences . . . the dance education profession can withstand the most intimate and extensive scrutiny" (p. 24). Another new development is the involvement of dance in the field of computer and information sciences; chapter 9 describes this in detail.

Despite these recent developments, observational techniques and research—whether qualitative (choreographic evaluation) or quantitative (dance technology)—are underutilized in the dance teaching profession. Dance teacher observation and evaluation have been limited to infrequent visits to student teachers in the field and have been notably devoid of appropriate tools and standards. Meanwhile, the relatively recent application of computer technology to the recording and analysis of human behaviors has resulted in the development of comprehensive catalogs of teaching behaviors, which can be assimilated by computer programs to produce quantifiable data. These programs not only objectively describe and interpret behavioral data, they prepare the data for sophisticated statistical analyses, which in turn generate valuable information about the teaching process.

This chapter shows how such a computer-aided recording and analysis system has been developed for and applied to dance instruction to produce unique ways of examining dance teaching. The chapter covers a review of the literature, the rationale behind the development of a dance teacher behavior catalog, a detailed four-dimensional dance teacher profile generated by the system, an additional technique for recording and analyzing dance teacher mobility, and a discussion of the uses of and implications for such dance teacher quantification procedures and findings.

Teacher Behavior Catalog

Prior studies of classroom behavior have principally, but not solely, dealt with verbal communication in a closed classroom in which students are usually seated. Dance teaching has been conspicuously absent from this series of studies. Until the 1970s, no attempt was made to identify the personality traits and attitudes of the dance teacher, to compare dance teacher behaviors with other teacher behaviors, or to develop a descriptive list of dance teacher actions that in turn would provide a basis for detailed dance teacher behavior analysis. Clearly, a dance teacher behavior catalog was needed.

Background

A survey of dance teaching literature—from Arbeau's *Orchesography* (1589/1967) to *The Chalif Text Book of Dancing* (Chalif, 1916) to contemporary dance education texts and unpublished research (Brauer, 1975; Hayes, 1964; Joyce, 1973; Stinson, 1985)—shows an emphasis on teacher traits, abilities, and personalities rather than on observable pedagogical behaviors and strategies. These behaviors and strategies exist in any instructional setting, but only since the 1970s have they been identified and recorded, most notably in two studies undertaken by dance researchers at the University of North Carolina. The first study (Lunt, 1974), attempted to establish acceptable construct validity and judge reliability standards and produced a system that showed promise in describing the teaching of choreography. It did not, however, establish any comprehensive category system of behaviors, which is a critical first step in any behavior observation system. The second study (Lord, 1981-1982) attempted to describe a system for observing and comparatively analyzing the teaching of choreography as opposed to validating observation reliability standards. Although Lord found that her system was a valid way of collecting data, her study was limited by its use of a small sample of dance teachers and the fact that her instrument was an adaption of a physical education teacher behavior model. Hence her findings were interpreted accordingly.

Unlike most other teaching disciplines, the teaching of dance is characterized by a wide range of nonverbal behaviors, yet literature on nonverbal teaching behaviors is minimal. Simon and Boyer's taxonomy (1974) lists 99 teacher observation instruments and studies, of which only 14 are concerned with the nonverbal aspects of teaching. Two studies dealt with psychomotor categories (Buehler & Richmond, 1963; Hall, 1963) but were socioanthropological in application. In physical education research, Anderson and Barrette (1978) published descriptive studies of nonverbal teaching behaviors, while Catelli (1979) referred to nonverbal moves in teaching physical education.

Because much of what dance teachers do is nonverbal, books on teaching dance tend to stress the qualitative and often intangible teaching behaviors. These books mention demonstrating, leading, developing concepts, using imagery, posing movement problems, manipulating limbs and torsos, and presenting facts and opinions as typical dance teaching behaviors.

For example, the literature describes behaviors such as "guides," "inspires," "challenges," and "encourages," which obviously are difficult to define. What is needed, then, is a comprehensive catalog of dance teacher behaviors that gives equal import to nonverbal behaviors, plus a behavior recording and analysis system that is suitable for dance and that can guarantee objective and supportable results. In the discussion that follows, such a system will be described—an original integration of observable dance teacher behaviors and effective recording and analysis technique.

Current Catalog

The current catalog (see Table 3.1) was prepared by a group of students who were directed to identify as closely as possible all the teacher's behaviors (as distinct from traits and attitudes) during a dance class. Another list of dance teacher behaviors was compiled from observations by the teacher's peers. Over 150 different behaviors resulted from collating these lists. The behaviors were then divided into five subgroups—verbal, nonverbal, cadential, gestural, and miscellaneous—and reduced in number to 60 to eliminate redundancy. Definitions were assigned for each behavior, and the subgroups were further reduced to three—verbal, nonverbal, and miscellaneous (the teacher's facings and proximity to students). Later a fourth subgroup, teacher location behaviors, was added. Finally, each behavior was assigned a label and given a function and a descriptor.

Table 3.1 Catalog of Dance Teacher Behaviors

Functions	Kinds	Key
1 Direct pedagogical	(V) Verbal	(S) Subject-Teacher
2 Indirect pedagogical	(NV) Nonverbal	(O) Object-Student(s)
3 Nonpedagogical	(M) Miscellaneous	
4 Counterpedagogical		

Label	Behavior	Function	Kind	Descriptor
A	Approaches	3	NV	S locates directly towards O.
AC	Accompanies	2	M	S accompanies a movement or maintains a rhythmic beat with an object other than own body (e.g., beats a drum).
AF	Affirms	2	V	S ratifies or confirms action by O (e.g., "OK," "Good!"). Usually this event is accompanied by a nod of the head.
AP	Apologizes	3	V	S makes an excuse for a fault. Usually starts event with, "I'm sorry . . ."
AQ	Asks Questions	3	V	S seeks information by soliciting a direct response (e.g., "How many triplets can you have in a two-four measure?").
C	Counts	1	V	S recites numerals to keep time by counting beats.
CA	Cautions	1	V	S warns O of pending danger or injury (e.g., "Avoid applying pressure to the knee").
CD	Cadence	1	M	S keeps time by sounds other than with an object or by counting (e.g., claps hands, clicks tongue or fingers).
CF	Confusion	2	M	S appears bewildered or puzzled.
CO	Corrects	1	V	S remedies or rectifies errors or faults in O's behavior.

Label	Behavior	Function	Kind	Descriptor
CR	Criticizes	1	V	S indicates errors or faults in O's behavior (e.g., "Your weight is not centered properly").
CU	Cues	1	V	S prompts by giving hints and reminders.
D	Demonstrates	1	NV	S illustrates or shows movement by exemplification while class observes.
DC	Develops Concepts	1	V	S gradually presents or discloses theoretical concepts of movement.
DI	Disciplines	3	V	S punishes or penalizes O (e.g., sends out of class).
E	Empathizes	2	V	S appears to experience empathy with O and expresses sincere understanding (e.g., "I understand how difficult this turn is").
G	Gestures	2	NV	S shows, expresses, or directs by motion of limb or body (e.g., points).
GD	Gives Directions	1	V	S gives instructions pertaining to orientation, termination, starting, or direction (e.g., "Start left," "Backwards").
GF	Gives Facts	1	V	S asserts, as accurate or established, certain information (e.g., "The deltoid is a thick, triangular muscle covering the shoulder and is used when raising the arm").
GO	Gives Opinion	3	V	S presents personal point of view.
I	Instructs	1	V	S furnishes O with instructions pertaining to skills and technique (e.g., "Begin the plié with hips rotated outward").
IC	Idiosyncratic Comment	3	NV	S displays speech characteristics peculiar to himself/herself (e.g., "OK," "Um," "Right," "Y' know").
ID	Identifies O	3	V	S recognizes O and refers to him/her by name.
IG	Idiosyncratic Gesture	3	NV	S displays a behavioral characteristic to himself/herself (e.g., bites nails, looks at watch).

Cont.

Table 3.1 (Continued)

Label	Behavior	Function	Kind	Descriptor
IV	Invites	2	V	S solicits participation, experimentation or effort. Usually begins with, "Let's try . . ." or, "Can you . . . ?"
J	Jokes	3	V	S speaks in fun, quips, or tells a joke.
L	Leads	1	NV	S shows the activity by performing it in front of O, while O follows.
Ll	Reclines	3	NV	S is in prostrate or recumbent position, supported by a surface that is usually horizontal.
LS	Listens	3	V	S pays silent attention to what O is saying.
M	Manages	2	V	S organizes or arranges the instructional environment (e.g., calls roll, operates turntable, reads class notes).
MA	Manually Assists	1	NV	S aids or adjusts O by moving/manipulating O's body or limbs with hands.
NE	Negative Expression	4	NV	S expresses negation, disagreement or disappointment, usually facially (e.g., frowns, shakes head from side to side).
O	Observes	3	NV	S watches O attentively.
P	Participates	2	NV	S takes part in activity without leading or demonstrating.
PE	Positive Expression	2	NV	S expresses praise or approval, usually with face (e.g., smiles, nods).
PO	Postures	3	NV	S assumes a pose (e.g., stands with arms folded or akimbo, leans on post).
PR	Praises	2	V	S expresses warm approval or admiration.
PV	Previews	1	V	S notifies O in advance of projected content or strategies (e.g., "Today we are going to explore intragroup spatial relationships").

Label	Behavior	Function	Kind	Descriptor
R	Runs	3	NV	S moves at a pace faster than a walk.
RE	Retreats	3	NV	S leaves or moves away from O.
RV	Reviews	1	V	S goes over or repeats the content or strategies that have been presented to O earlier (e.g., "You recall that last time we added the axial movement to the locomotion pattern").
S	Stands	3	NV	S maintains an upright position on his/her feet.
SA	Sarcasm	4	V	S makes caustic or contemptuous remarks (e.g., taunts O).
SC	Self-corrects	3	V	S remedies or rectifies errors in own behavior (e.g., "I started with the wrong beat").
SI	Sits	3	NV	S rests with the body supported on the buttocks.
SL	Silence	3	V	S is not making any vocal sounds.
SN	Sings	3	M	S utters words or sounds in musical tones. Includes humming, chanting, and intoning.
U	Uses Props	3	NV	S uses an inanimate object for instructional purposes (e.g., blackboard, ropes, bone pads). *Note*—not for cadence or management).
UI	Uses Imagery	1	V	S uses metaphors or similes to motivate or illustrate a movement or movement concept (e.g., "Feel your arm float down like a feather").
V	Volume	3	M	Loudness of S's voice. VL (loud), VM (moderate), VS (soft).
W	Walks	3	NV	S travels on foot by steps.

Note. Catalog of Dance Teacher Behaviors by J.A. Gray, 1984, *Journal of Teaching in Physical Education*, **3**(2), pp. 75-78. Copyright 1984 by *Journal of Teaching in Physical Education*. Adapted by permission.

Classification of teaching behaviors.   The functions were called *direct pedagogical*, *indirect pedagogical*, *nonpedagogical*, and *counterpedagogical*, labels based on the degree to which the particular behavior served the instructional purpose. Direct pedagogical behaviors directly impart knowledge or give direction, for example, "instructs" or "demonstrates." Indirect pedagogical teacher behaviors leave room for student interpretation, such as "gestures" or "affirms." Nonpedagogical behaviors neither promote nor hinder the teaching/learning process, while counterpedagogical behaviors are inappropriate and hinder or damage the instructional process. The descriptors are discrete, succinct definitions of each behavior that ensure teacher behaviors cannot be confused and do not overlap.

Hardware and software.   The catalog of dance teacher behaviors was designed to be compatible with the keyboard, conventions, and syntax of the SSR System 7—a sophisticated computer-based recording and analysis system. The catalog can be used, however, without computer technology support. Several less expensive systems are available for collecting and sorting teacher behaviors, and these include checklist and timeline systems. The SSR System 7 is a method for encoding data in real time for subsequent transcription by a computer. It was designed in 1975 by Gordon Stephenson, D.P.R. Smith, and Tom Roberts at the University of Wisconsin at Madison and has been used extensively by zoologists, psychologists, sociologists, and pediatricians to record and analyze sociobehavioral situations. It was originally designed to follow the behaviors of monkeys in the Madison zoo's primate colony. The dance teacher behavior research presented here represents the first application of this technology to educational investigation.

The System's hardware consists of an electronic keyboard for entering behavioral events, a tape recorder for recording keyboard output, a playback tape deck, a signal conditioning circuit, and a small computer. The equipment has been updated to include a personal computer that is adapted to process all input data and display it directly onto a monitor screen. The software consists of a grammar processing program called Plexyn, also designed by Stephenson, Smith, and Roberts, which transcribes, times, and organizes the encoded data and effectively readies it for statistical analysis. The software is unique in that it is capable of handling parallel arrays of data when the user wants to categorize different behavioral subgroups—in this case, verbal, nonverbal, orientation, and location—from the same behavioral sequence, thus allowing analyses across multiple dimensions.

Use of the Catalog

The catalog and recording system were successfully used to generate detailed four-dimensional behavioral profiles of several dance teachers. The following describes the generation of a profile.

Procedures

For this profile verbal, nonverbal, orientation, and location dimensions were studied. The subject was a female ballet teacher with fifteen years of teaching experience. Her teaching behaviors were recorded onto videotape to allow verification and consistency. Her teaching was noninvasively monitored in a ballet studio setting by use of two video cameras. One of the cameras, which was mounted high on the wall and had an extra wide lens, recorded location and proxemic behaviors. The other camera monitored the teacher's nonverbal behaviors. In addition, she wore a small wireless microphone, which recorded all her verbal behaviors. After the recording session, the tapes were played back and the behaviors were encoded, or entered into the computer via one- or two-letter coding labels. The entries occurred in real time with each pass being synchronized, and each dimension was encoded separately. The Plexyn program converted the encoded data into short strings of characters prefaced by time and frame counts. Each of the four data files later underwent detailed statistical analysis and the results were formatted for easy interpretation.

Results

The results were categorized in four distinct aspects of the teaching process, enabling the researchers to isolate formerly indistinguishable components. These dimensions of the teaching process were analyzed and interpreted as follows.

Verbal. As expected, the dominant verbal behavior displayed by the subject was "instruction," most of which was directed to the class as a whole. The ballet teacher displayed a ratio of 1:3 between correcting students on specific errors and correcting all the students on errors of a more general nature, thereby illustrating a balance of attention to movement detail. Overall, the teacher verbalized approximately half of the time which concurs with Lord's study (1981-1982) and reinforces the notion that dance teachers use a disproportionately limited amount of nonverbal behaviors to communicate their art form.

Implications and questions about dance teacher training curriculum now arise. Is this finding, which has been borne out by research, taken into consideration when planning course content and curriculum design for dance teachers? In this study the verbal behaviors also accounted for a higher percentage of direct pedagogical influence than the nonverbal ones, indicating that the spoken word is still the dominant method for communicating the knowledge and skills of dance.

Nonverbal. "Leading," "demonstrating," and "manually assisting" accounted for 40 percent of all the nonverbal behaviors recorded. This suggests that the teaching in this session was characterized by modeling and mirroring—

teaching behaviors whose importance and effectiveness are unique to dance. A small amount of time was spent on "gesturing," while "posturing" and "managing the environment" (moving equipment, changing tapes, calling roll) were used the least. "Observing" was included as an indirectly pedagogical behavior and accounted for a significant amount of teaching time, which raises the question of the worth of this behavior and uncovers further concerns regarding the training of our dance teachers. Are we including observational skills in our dance teacher preparation programs? If so, are we investigating alternative methods of observation including the latest surveillance technology and appropriate techniques from other disciplines?

Orientation. Recording and analyzing the students' physical relationships with the dance teacher resulted in a clearer picture of where the teacher's behaviors were most often directed. The teacher usually addressed the students by observing or facing them, and as she was moving much of the time, her proximity to the students varied. Nonetheless, the study concluded that physical proximity can be an important and effective dance teaching strategy.

The teacher in this study faced only half of the students at any given time, which is not unusual considering the configuration of most dance studios and the tendency for most teachers to instruct from the front center area. This "podium" orientation of dance teachers is typical of most other teaching disciplines and is evidence of the strong influence of the traditional classroom model on dance teaching. Fortunately, the dance studio or moving space lends itself to other orientations, such as teaching within a circle of students, between rows of students, and on the perimeter of the space, as in ballet classes when the students work at the ballet barre.

The orientation of dance teaching has a powerful, but as yet unmeasured, influence on the teaching/learning process. In sum, the high incidence of directly facing or observing individual students suggests a willingness on the teacher's part to maintain and promote positive teacher/student interaction. In addition, both her close-range and long-range proximity to students indicated accessibility and visibility, two vital variables that warrant closer study and measurement.

Location. The location dimension, which represents the whereabouts of the teacher, is recorded graphically by the computer on a cellular matrix so that the teacher's locomotory patterns can be visually registered and evaluated. In this study, the ballet teacher circulated throughout almost 90 percent of the available space, reinforcing the accessibility variable found in the orientation dimension summary. Accessibility was also supported by the low variance measure, that is, her locating behaviors were evenly distributed in time and space. She spent a great amount of intermittent time close to the source of sound accompaniment, which suggests that she preferred to establish a focal point for the students from which she could supervise and direct the class. The space immediately in front of this focal point accounted for much of her movement and appeared to represent the area most conducive to learning for students. Corners were the most neglected areas and should be avoided by students.

Implications of Findings

This four-dimensional behavioral profile of a dance teacher has value for the teacher herself in terms of self-awareness and self-evaluation. The quantified findings show that she was assertive, active, confident, and well-prepared. She demonstrated a concern for individual students while at the same time challenging the class to learn the dance material. She was quite accessible to students, although she directed the class from a relatively small podium area in front of the class. Her verbal and nonverbal behaviors were well-balanced, yet the sheer volume of verbal behaviors suggests that dance teaching employs an unusually high proportion of verbal cues and instructions to impart information about a nonverbal art form. This finding contradicts the widely-held notion that dance teaching is largely nonverbal.

Following is a more complete discussion about dance teacher location patterns and mobility factors.

Assessment of Dance Teacher Mobility

The technique for recording and analyzing dance teacher mobility that is discussed in this section assumes that a teacher's mobility pattern constitutes an important dimension of the dance teaching/learning process and further assumes that this dimension is critical to understanding and improving teaching effectiveness. This section of the chapter describes the development and application of a computer-assisted tracking system for recording, analyzing, and reproducing the location patterns of dance teachers (see Figure 3.1). The terms *mobility*, *location*, and *locomotion* will be used interchangeably. The methodology that is presented here was designed to provide precise, objective measures of the dance teacher's position in space and time. In this investigation, the location behaviors were electronically recorded and then transcribed and analyzed by computer. The overall result was a technically sound and advanced monitoring system that can be used in pedagogical settings in any discipline, although it was originally designed for dance instruction.

This technique, which is still exploratory in nature, is primarily concerned with describing and examining the phenomena of location rather than with testing hypotheses about the relationship between location behavior and the dance teaching environment or between teacher mobility and teaching effectiveness. More teacher mobility relationships worthy of scientific study can be found in the conceptual framework in chapter 2. Meanwhile, we will examine the literature pertaining to teaching and mobility.

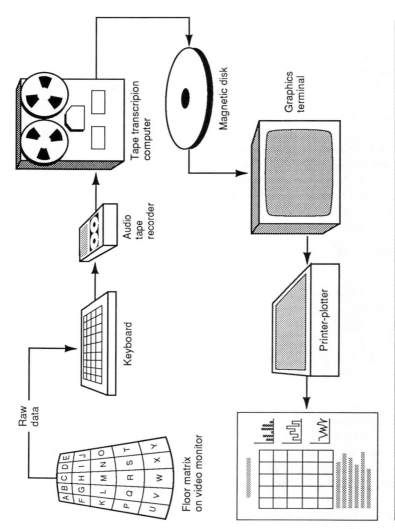

Figure 3.1. Computer-aided hardware system for tracking dance teacher location behaviors. *Note.* From "A Computerized Technique for Recording and Analyzing Teacher Mobility" by J.A. Gray, 1984, *Educational Studies*, **10**(1), p. 24. Copyright 1984 by *Educational Studies*. Adapted by permission.

Development of Current Technique

Teaching typically takes place in an environment that has been designed or adapted to facilitate some range of teacher movement. Teachers display a wide range of teaching behaviors in response to this environment and in addition must negotiate the spatial variables in order to teach more effectively. While students are expected to remain relatively stationary or to move only within established limits, the teacher is permitted to roam and generally appears active and accessible by means of location behaviors. Thus, it is surprising that few research studies have investigated the locomotory behaviors of teachers; until the early 1980's no such studies existed at all in the dance literature. Research studies in other teaching disciplines, while limited in value for dance education, are reviewed here because of their methodologies.

Adams and Biddle (1970) found while studying social studies and mathematics classes that a teacher's age affected his or her location behaviors. They also discovered that teachers spent 70 percent of their time at the front of the classroom with the remaining time divided between walking around the periphery of the room and visiting central areas. A simple nonanalytic tool for recording teacher location is found in physical education literature (Barrette, 1977), but it has not been developed into a reliable research procedure. In other studies, teacher movements and proxemics have been investigated in studies of nonverbal communication in the classroom (Galloway, 1970), but again no trustworthy method exists to monitor or measure actual teacher pathways. Well-documented location tracking systems exist in animal behavior research (Crawley, Szaras, Pryor, Creveling, & Bernard, 1982; Rosenblum, 1979; Stephenson, 1979) and in infant behavior research (Ainsworth & Wittig, 1969). The technique presented here is unique in that it can observe and measure dance teacher location behaviors by utilizing a cleverly designed computer-aided system. It was tested not in traditional classrooms but in dance studios at the University of Wisconsin-Madison.

Procedure.   Because human mobility patterns are measured in space and time, a manageable floor matrix had to be constructed with a sufficient number of cells to generate meaningful location behavior data. Data was recorded in three spacious dance studios, which had wooden floors, high studs, and natural lighting. Floor markings facilitated the construction of a 5 × 5 matrix (totaling 25 cells) for coding and recording purposes. The 25 matrix cells were coded A-Y (see Figure 3.2).

The teaching sessions were recorded by a wide-lens video camera mounted 10 feet from the floor, which was able to capture the entire moving space. The tapes were later played back on a video monitor while trained observers recorded in real time the teacher's movements from cell to cell. Intraobserver reliability and interobserver objectivity were 92 percent and 91 percent respectively. The encoded data was then processed by a small computer—a

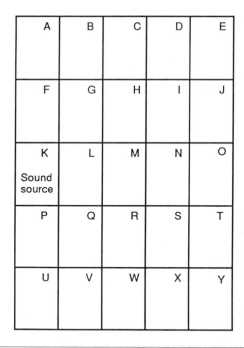

A	B	C	D	E
F	G	H	I	J
K Sound source	L	M	N	O
P	Q	R	S	T
U	V	W	X	Y

Figure 3.2. Location matrix. *Note.* From "A Computerized Technique for Recording and Analyzing Teacher Mobility" by J.A. Gray, 1984, *Educational Studies*, **10**(1), p. 25. Copyright 1984 by *Educational Studies*. Adapted by permission.

PDP-11/20—and the more powerful Harris Data Craft 6024/5. Plexyn, the software that was employed to process the verbal and nonverbal dance teacher behaviors, was used to transcribe, time, and organize the data. Plexyn was able to draw on user-defined values of the location coding properties to verify, complete, and uniformly format the data entries in the observers' record for subsequent statistical analysis.

Analysis. The data, organized by Plexyn, were stored on a computer disc. For analysis purposes, multiple indicators of the location behaviors were developed. They were quantified as follows:

1. Mean incidence per cell
2. Mean duration per cell
3. Total number of cell changes
4. Total number of empty cells
5. Total distance traveled
6. Mean distance from source of sound accompaniment
7. Left/right orientation
8. Rate of cell change per minute

A Versatec electrostatic plotter was used to graphically represent the actual linear pathways of the teachers. Both the location measures and the mobility patterns for each dance teacher appeared on a video display monitor and then were printed out as hard copy. Selected location measures were printed out as histograms and accompanied the graphic pathway depiction (see Figure 3.3).

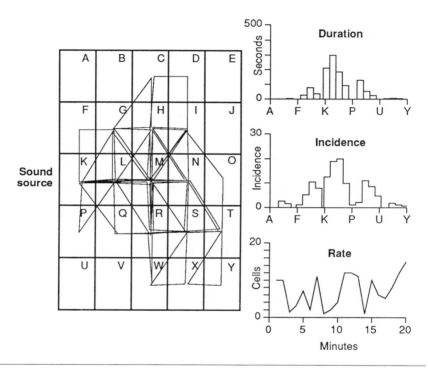

Figure 3.3. Graphic and histograms showing dance teacher location patterns. *Note.* From "A Computerized Technique for Recording and Analyzing Teacher Mobility" by J.A. Gray, 1984, *Educational Studies,* **10**(1), p. 28. Copyright 1984 by *Educational Studies.* Adapted by permission.

Findings. The computer and electronic accessories allowed the user to encode dance teacher mobility sequences in real time with a minimum of observer error or interference, thus drastically reducing the human error factor common to most observational situations. It eliminated the subjective "gut feeling" approach to behavioral observation analysis and simplified the normally complex analysis of a large number of variables. As dance teaching has possibly the highest mobility component of any teaching discipline, it is fitting that the dance field developed this prototype location tracking system for teaching.

Implications.   The results of this exploratory research suggest that information on observed dance teacher location behaviors may be an important parameter when studying the variations within dance teacher populations. A correlation analysis could provide both a model and perspective from which to evaluate dance teacher behavior and to make predictions about variations. The continued study of the quantitative aspects of dance teacher mobility can create a vantage point for the study of the entire dance teaching/learning process.

Exploration of other aspects of location and their effect on education are beyond the scope of this chapter but well within the capabilities of the technique. Further research should consider the relationship between dance teacher location and such variables as class size and composition, teaching fatigue, teacher motivation, student and teacher feedback systems, and dance teacher variability. Experimental studies could be designed to determine if certain measures of mobility, such as rates of cell change, are typical in classes for slow learners or beginners, and if so, how they are related to student learning. Other dance studies might be designed to test whether dance teacher mobility is related to teacher accessibility, especially in terms of the student's perception of that accessibility. Time/series studies might ascertain whether mobility changes at a specific point in the series and might determine mobility trends over time (i.e., increases, decreases, and episodes, with or without modification or intervention). Mobility patterns of dance teachers could be compared across content areas (e.g., jazz, folk dance, improvisation), grade or age levels, time of day, and size of the dance teaching space. Once certain measures of mobility are positively correlated with certain measures of learning, these findings could be incorporated in preservice and in-service dance teacher training programs.

This technically advanced methodology for tracking and quantifying dance teacher location behaviors provides opportunities to investigate critical relationships that occur in dance pedagogical settings and apply them to improving dance teaching. The possible uses of both the profiling and the mobility tracking systems are now examined.

Uses of the Catalog and Mobility Assessment

Explorations with the dance profiling and tracking procedures have revealed the following possible uses in the dance education field:

- Developing dance students' perceptive skills regarding their own teaching behaviors
- Using experienced dance teachers' behavioral and mobility profiles as models
- Evaluating dance teaching objectively and scientifically

- Explaining and predicting the dance teaching process by discovering the laws that operate in dance pedagogical settings
- Improving dance teaching strategies and effectiveness
- Identifying and practicing dance teaching patterns and episodes that best suit the dance content
- Testing dance teaching assumptions
- Generating hypotheses that will build scientific and artistic knowledge about the field of dance education

Conclusions

The development of a catalog of dance teacher behaviors plus computerized profiling systems for recording and analyzing behaviors represents the first step in what promises to become an extensive and profound investigation of the dance teaching process. These methodologies allow dance educators and researchers to explore and employ tools that not only test dance teaching assumptions but also generate many hypotheses by virtue of their computerization, storage capacities, and speed. More about the advances of computer technology and dance is presented in chapter 9. Meanwhile, it is important to note that while dance is yet a young science, it has entered the arena of scientific investigation at a time when information technology is being revolutionized. For dance educators, this means that our questions are no longer impossible to answer. Our demands and queries need no longer be bound by the infinite and vague horizons of the arts nor the rigid structure and syntax of the sciences. For dance education, this means that powerful tools and techniques are available for investigation of hypotheses. Indeed, the new technological applications may determine the directions of future dance teaching and learning research.

Regardless of research findings, many dance teachers will continue to teach in ways that they find personally or professionally appropriate and satisfying. Some dance teachers have devised unique ways to approach their teaching responsibilities and present material to students. In chapter 4, a selection of different instructional points of view is presented and discussed.

Key Terms

Behavioral profile—an outline of a person's behavioral characteristics

Catalog—a systemized list with descriptions of items

Counterpedagogical—teaching that is inappropriate and counterproductive

Descriptor—a word used to identify an item in an information retrieval system

Directly pedagogical—teaching that is directly related to transmitting information

Histogram—a graphic representation of a frequency distribution

Indirectly pedagogical—teaching that is indirectly or incidentally related to transmitting information

Interobserver objectivity—several observers in objective agreement

Intraobserver reliability—each observer's own consistency in recording events or actions

Location—the specification of position and boundaries

Matrix—a network of intersections

Mobility—capability of moving from place to place or locomoting

Mobility profile—an outline of a person's locomotory patterns

Nonpedagogical—teaching that is neutral or noncommital

Nonverbal behaviors—physical actions and reactions of persons

Observation—attentively watching an event or action

Orientation—a person's position and facing in respect to a reference system

Plexyn—a computer application that can process recorded behavioral data

Source of sound accompaniment—the location of the sound or music for a dance class

Verbal behaviors—words and sounds

Student Activities and Assignments

1. Design a catalog for the study of dance teacher accessibility. Consider which teacher behaviors and learner behaviors you would include.
2. Explain what is meant by "multiple indicators" in the descriptive study of dance teaching. Outline a possible dance teacher research project that incorporates this concept.
3. Locate a recent taxonomy of teacher behavior research. Compare the number of non-verbal behavioral studies with verbal ones. Contrast this ratio with an earlier edition of the same book and list the current trends.
4. "If it exists, it can be measured." Discuss this statement as it applies to the scientific study of dance teaching.
5. Create a chronological bibliographic file of dance teacher and dance teaching research and sort it into two categories—qualitative and quantitative. Identify any trends in these areas of research.

Further Reading

Gray, A. (1984). A catalog of dance teacher behaviors. *Journal of Teaching Physical Education*, **3**(2), 71-80.

Lord, M. (1981-1982). A characterization of dance teacher behavior in choreography and technique classes. *Dance Research Journal*, **14**(1 & 2), 15-24.

Stephenson, G.R., & Roberts, T.W. (1977). The SSR System 7: A general encoding system with computerized transcription. *Behavioral Research Methods and Instrumentation*, **9**, 434-441.

Chapter 4

Instructional Perspectives

Chapter 3 was devoted to dance teaching and dance teachers, but paid only passing attention to the individual signature that dance teachers typically place on their own teaching style and approach. A teacher's method is in large part dependent upon her or his own training and dance experiences and also upon the teaching environment and the ability and number of the students being taught. Teaching style and methods are enhanced and often distinguished by the teacher's own point of view or perspective.

This chapter presents some different instructional perspectives that have been construed to facilitate the teaching and learning of dance. These perspectives are more concerned with ways of presenting the dance materials rather than with what is being presented. Dance instructional perspectives are discrete methodologies for teaching dance, which are typically characterized by a point of view that may be philosophical, emotional, scientific, or experience-based. These perspectives can be classified graphically along vertical and horizontal axes based on who makes instructional decisions during a dance class (see Figure 4.1). In this graphic model the teacher can make all the decisions (*command* mode), or the students can make the decisions (*inventive* mode). When both the students and the teacher share the decisions equally, the mode is *interactive*. Should neither the teacher nor the students accept responsibility for decision making, a *counteractive* mode is present.

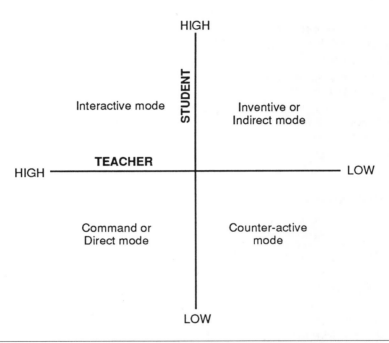

Figure 4.1. Instructional modes for dance (with level of responsibility for decision making indicated on each axis).

The command mode is typical of most technique classes, such as ballet and jazz, when a direct teaching method is the most effective way to teach stylized dance technique (i.e., the refinement and mastery of steps, positions, and routines or phrases). Dance teachers who employ this mode often teach as they were taught themselves and rely on imitation and mirror reflections. The inventive mode results when students explore, select, and use their own movement ideas. The teacher's role in this mode is facilitative and supportive; she may pose the movement problems to be solved or establish appropriate parameters within which the students make most or all of the decisions. When the class consists of an equal interchange of ideas and decisions, the interactive mode is present. This is the most dynamic of the modes and tends to lead to the greatest levels of creativity, achievement, and satisfaction. A counteractive mode represents a breakdown of student/teacher relations. When nobody takes responsibility for decisions in a dance class, apathy, frustration, and hostility result.

The remainder of this chapter focuses on three instructional perspectives, each of which features a unique way of looking at and organizing the full complement of dance material. The first of these perspectives employs a "time engaged in dancing" approach to dance instruction and is quantitative in focus. The second perspective is based on a selection of commonly-used metaphors for the human body. Designed by Carol Lynne Moore, it has been reproduced here because of its insight and implications for dance instruction. The third perspective is represented by Barbara Mettler's polarity theory of dance instruction, which explores organizing and teaching dance via movement and nonmovement extremes, a common practice in many creative dance, structured improvisation, composition, and movement analysis classes. In sum, this chapter views the teaching and learning of dance from three different views—quantitative, metaphoric, and polar.

Quantitative Perspective

The lack of research in the area of dance teacher and learner interactions indicates a lack of appropriate tools rather than a lack of concern. These interactions are best measured by academic learning time (ALT) or time on task (TOT) techniques. Although many ALT and TOT studies have been reported in other disciplines—physical education and mathematics, for example—none have been conducted in dance. ALT researchers generally agree that increased learning time increases learning. In other words, when a teacher devotes most of his or her time to direct instruction and the students are involved in direct learning, greater achievement and improvement result. In dance, this conclusion can be applied to mean that when teachers actively facilitate students' engagement in dance, they increase the opportunity to learn and as a result, greater learning and understanding takes place.

As the learning mode is dependent on the teaching mode, researchers believe that optimum learning takes place when both the dance teacher and the students are involved in appropriate teaching and learning behaviors. The following theoretical study shows that by using a proficient systematic behavior recording and analysis system, dance researchers can identify and apply their findings to improve and enhance individual instructional styles and dance courses.

Procedure

Teacher and learner behaviors are recorded by two synchronized video cameras, one focused on the dance teacher and the other mounted on the wall at a height of about 10 feet. The mounted camera is equipped with a wide angle lens in order to capture the actions of all the students in class. The teacher has attached to her clothing a small wireless microphone, which transmits all her verbal behaviors to a receiver on one of the cameras. After one or more of the teacher's classes have been recorded, the videotapes are played back on separate monitors. Using one- or two-letter coding labels previously assigned to the behaviors under observation, the teaching and learning episode is encoded and recorded onto a magnetic tape by an electronic keyboard that allows for real-time input. The keyboard is attached to a high speed playback deck and a signal conditioning circuit. The entire encoding system, designed by Gordon Stephenson and Tom Roberts (1977), is controlled by computer, which processes the recorded data with software especially designed for transcribing, timing, and organizing the encoded data. The management software comprises a grammar processing program called Plexyn, also designed by Stephenson and Roberts (1977). Plexyn is a complex syntax analyzer that draws upon user-defined values of the coding properties to verify, complete, and uniformly format the entries in the observer's record. The original observed behavioral data is rendered analyzable, that is, it is timed and managed so that the teacher and learner behaviors can be either independently analyzed or merged for comparative analysis.

Instructional behaviors.   The dance teacher behaviors that are recorded by this system are divided into two categories—appropriate and inappropriate (see Figure 4.2). Appropriate behaviors directly or indirectly influence learning. Inappropriate behaviors are considered counterpedagogical, that is, they have no bearing on the teaching and learning of dance. Examples are neglect, sarcasm, and physical or sexual abuse. All behaviors are recorded as verbal or nonverbal.

Learning behaviors.   Dance learner behaviors are also divided into two categories—appropriate and inappropriate (see Figure 4.3). These categories are further divided into behaviors that involve movement and those that involve stillness. Appropriate movement behaviors can be axial or locomotory, while appropriate stillness behaviors can be classified as attending (e.g., listening) or inputting (responding to a question). Inappropriate behaviors can be off-task or neutral. Apathy and tardiness are off-task student behaviors.

Analysis of Data

Statistical analysis, also performed by computer, reveals a number of interesting data bases and data characteristics. These are summarized as follows:

1. Incidence of the behaviors—the number of times each behavior occurs during the class

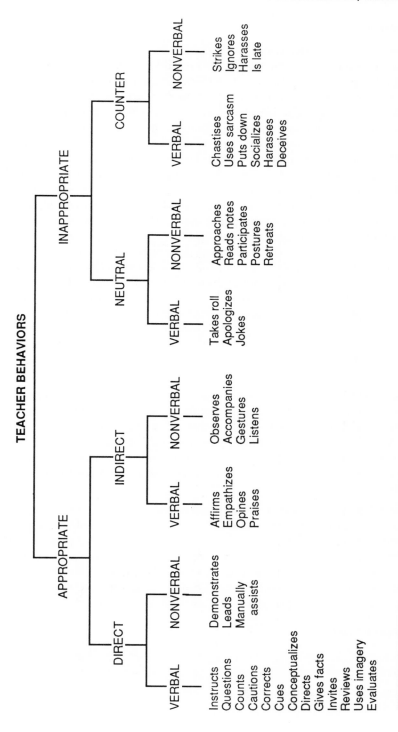

Figure 4.2. Appropriate and inappropriate teacher behaviors.

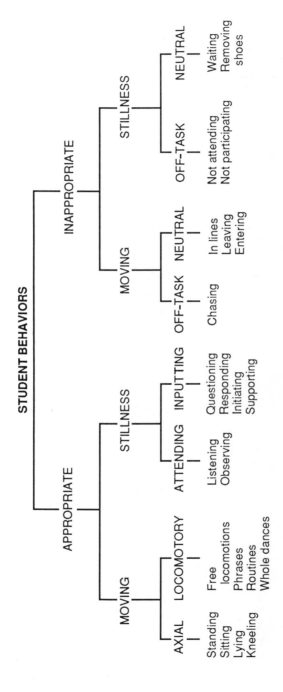

Figure 4.3. Appropriate and inappropriate student behaviors.

2. Duration of the behaviors—the exact amount of time spent on each behavior
3. Episodic nature of the behaviors—whether behaviors occur, recur, or form cyclic patterns
4. Absence of behaviors—the fact that some behaviors do not occur

Thus the computer, using quantification strategies, produces information on the amount of actual teaching and learning time and subsequently analyzes the relationship between the time engaged in teaching dance and the time engaged in learning dance (Gray, 1986). The time engaged in teaching dance (TETD) is calculated as the total percentage of the allotted teaching time that is occupied by direct, indirect, or neutral instructional behaviors. Teachers are ranked as "high engaged" when their percentage is 80 or above and "low engaged" when it falls below 80 percent. Direct teaching behaviors are weighted slightly more than indirect and neutral behaviors. Time engaged in learning dance (TELD) is similarly calculated and is comprised of the percentage of time students are actively engaged in appropriate moving and nonmoving activities and behaviors. Students who spend 80 percent or more of their time in these dance activities are regarded as high engaged while those who spent less time on task are considered low engaged.

Plotting the Results

The SSR software application called Summary Statistics is used to determine relationship coefficients within groups of teachers and students and between these groups. Further statistical analyses produce numerical information, which is reproduced as charts or graphs. For the purposes of this research, the results are plotted on the sectors of a specially designed quadrant that visually illustrates the array of teaching/learning situations (see Figure 4.4).

1. Quadrant One (Q1) comprises situations in which the teacher is high engaged and the students are high engaged. This is labeled a *collaborative* situation as a high percentage of appropriate teaching and learning behaviors occur. This situation is characterized by effective teaching behaviors and strategies fueled by a high level of student involvement, resulting in a sense of working together to achieve educational and artistic goals.
2. Quadrant Two (Q2) represents situations in which the teacher is high engaged and the students are low engaged. A high percentage of appropriate teacher behaviors combined with a high percentage of inappropriate student behaviors characterizes the *brick wall* dance instructional situation. The students display low involvement in the learning process and are rarely on task. The teacher, meanwhile, appears to be adequately teaching the material, but is faced with poor or no student response. The teacher finds him- or herself "up against a brick wall."

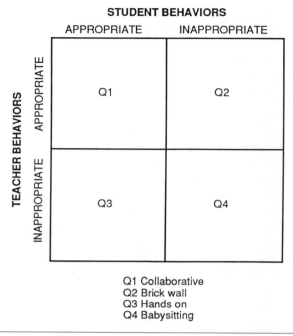

STUDENT BEHAVIORS

Q1 Collaborative
Q2 Brick wall
Q3 Hands on
Q4 Babysitting

Figure 4.4.   Instructional situations in dance.

3. Quadrant Three (Q3) represents situations in which the teacher is low engaged and the students are high engaged. Situations that fall into Q3 are characterized by a high percentage of student learning behaviors and a low percentage of appropriate teacher behaviors. This may be referred to as a *hands-on* situation because the students are working on task and are probably self-directed and self-motivated. The teacher, meanwhile, is displaying behaviors that are only minimally related to the teaching process.

4. Quadrant Four (Q4) represents situations in which both the teacher and the students are low engaged. Neither teacher nor students display adequate percentages of appropriate behaviors. Consequently, learning is unlikely to occur; the teacher is present but noninvolved. This situation is called *babysitting*.

Implications for Dance Instruction

Each instructional situation comprises a methodology (ways and means of teaching and learning) and a climate (mood and atmosphere). The Q1, or collaborative, situation reflects an ideal methodology for successful transmission of dance material to students. In this situation the teacher is prepared, enthusiastic, and committed to the artistic, intellectual, and cultural education of the students. At the same time, the students are motivated, curious, and willing to explore, practice, and learn. It is hoped that this climate prevails in most dance instruction settings. Most difficult and frustrating is the brick wall situation, in which the students are unwilling or unable to respond in an appropriate learning manner despite the teacher's competence and appropriate teaching behaviors. This situation may occur when a student teacher or substitute teacher is in charge or when the learners are opposed to dancing or are learning disabled. Methodology may be at fault, or the dance material may be too difficult or too easy, bringing about a brick wall climate.

The Q3, or hands-on, situation can be regarded as positive or negative. A situation in which students are actively engaged in learning activities despite the teacher's lack of appropriate instructional behaviors may be considered positive. However, students' involvement in learning may be only short-term in this situation, such as rehearsing for a dance production. During dance-making lessons, students may work independently on their creative projects without the teacher intervening, monitoring, or even observing. In this instance, teacher behaviors may seem minimal yet students are learning a great deal. The subsequent climate is characterized by autonomous, harmonious activity.

The Q4, or babysitting, climate is an intolerable and wasteful situation in which the teacher has little or no control and the students are constantly off-task. Appropriate teaching behaviors are replaced by inappropriate behaviors such as socializing or ignoring, and the students do as they please or don't do anything at all. This situation is evident when teachers spend most of their teaching time maintaining order, meting discipline, being distracted, or dismissing the dance class early as punishment. A kind of anarchist climate prevails.

Some dance teachers will not fall strictly into any one quadrant and teach accordingly. Typically, teachers shift from one methodology and climate to another, depending upon factors such as class level, dance topic, past experience, or external pressures. Teachers agree, however, that the collaborative situation is the most effective and desirable. Dance teachers are responsible for promoting the aesthetic, creative, intellectual, and cultural education of students through the medium of dance. To this end, it is critical that teachers execute optimal instructional behaviors and strategies and that students are afforded the greatest opportunity to engage in dance learning using appropriate learning behaviors.

In this discussion , four distinct dance instructional situations emerge from the quantification of dance teaching and learning behaviors using a computerized observation and analysis system. The accuracy of the results and subsequent quadrant application allows both teachers and students of dance to critically take stock of their respective interactive behavioral profiles. This method of identifying instructional situations for dance leads to constructive self-analysis and improved learning environments for dance. It is important to remember, however, that although a quantitative perspective points out strengths and weaknesses in dance instruction, it does not substitute for quality instruction.

Metaphoric Perspective

Social sciences have long recognized that one's self-image profoundly affects all aspects of one's life, from social relations to occupational achievement to the basic stability of psychic functioning (Wylie & MacGregor, 1951). Carol Lynne Moore (1985) believes that body image, shared consciously or unconsciously by the teacher and student, significantly influences all aspects of movement education as it occurs in the studio, gym, or playground. These global images, or body metaphors, color and shape instructional philosophy and curriculum. Often what is thought of as a mere common sense or as an established scientific fact is in reality the outgrowth of a tacitly accepted, traditional *weltanschauung* (world view). What has been strongly sensed, yet seldom intellectually acknowledged, is that athletes, dancers, sports medicine practioners, biomechanics researchers, and body therapists actually think, feel, talk, and act about their bodies in very different ways. Such differing and unexamined world views with contrasting body metaphors have created hidden but potent impediments to cross-disciplinary understanding and integration. They are responsible, at least in part, for the disagreements and schisms among the closely related fields of movement inquiry, education, and therapy. Therefore, each group must become aware of its salient metaphor(s) in order to transcend its subculture, "and this can be done only by making explicit the rules by which it operates" (Hall, 1977, p. 55). The next section discusses a few prevalent body metaphors and their implications in dance and movement education. The metaphors in these cases can be grouped together to form an instructional platform for dance—a metaphoric perspective.

The Body as Beast

In this metaphoric view, the body is thought of as an animal, usually a beast of burden, with a willful spirit that must be broken (see Figure 4.5). The body, like a pack mule, is meant to be worked hard and treated roughly—cajoled, prodded, driven with blows if necessary. The mode of instruction that arises out of this metaphor is typically found in sports but also in dance and emphasizes repetition and strain. The same sequence is repeated until the student "gets it right." Dance exercises that utilize pushing and pulling or increasing and holding muscle tension, as in certain adagio dance sequences, are also common. The instructor is the master, like an animal trainer, and the methods of instruction include exhortation ("Try harder!"), persuasion ("You can do it!"), prodding, and even ridicule. As we admire the traits of strength and endurance in beasts of burden, so do we aspire to them in the human body.

Yet carried to the extreme, dance instruction based on this metaphor can be injurious and dangerous. First, the instructor can simply overwork the student. Secondly, the student may learn to mistrust the kinesthetic feedback of his or her own body, and to see sensitivity as a sign of weakness. A fine line exists between repetition that yields mastery and fatigued repetition that engenders frustration and reinforces bad habits. Similarly, a delicate qualitative difference exists between muscular tension that builds strength and stresses that actually damage the muscles, ligaments, or tendons. Students and instructors who think of their bodies as beasts of burden are more likely to ignore these fine lines and qualitative differences in sensation. One of the corollaries of the metaphorical premise is that while the body is lazy and dumb like an beast, the mind is active and smart. This leads to the third danger, that successful training perpetuates the mind/body dichotomy rather than facilitating holistic integration of human functions. This can easily trigger a self-fulfilling, defeating prophecy: If one treats one's body as a lazy, stupid beast of burden to be closely controlled and kept in bounds by a whip, reins, yoke, or bribes, then that is what one's body becomes. The body has to be continually in training, and the total organism is seldom entrusted to the allegedly active mind. In this sense the situation resembles the next metaphor.

Figure 4.5.   Body as beast. *Note.*   Illustration courtesy of J. Allan Wellman.

The Body as Machine

In this view the body is regarded as a sleek, well-designed, efficient engine (see Figure 4.6). If the machine has a sufficient supply of energy and receives proper maintenance, it will continue running with a minimum of attention from the operator, in this case, the mind. The mind, like the driver of a car, is present mainly to turn the machine on and off, to steer, and to attend to wear and tear before parts actually break down. Otherwise, the machine goes through its preassigned motions automatically and precisely. This metaphor reflects our industrial and technological society—"machine-like bodies inhabiting a machine-like world" (Dossey, 1982, p. 14). The machine metaphor, likewise, lends itself to medical and biomedical research. What is the best sort of fuel for this engine? What is the right sort of compression-ignition ratio to keep neurons firing at maximum power and speed? What is the optimal angle of thrust for each of the bony levers? Not surprisingly, this world view, to a greater extent than other body metaphors, eagerly incorporates scientific findings into its instructional methods. Research fads affect such aspects of the dancer's life as nutrition, training duration, and even clothing worn. The training method itself is designed to program the machine properly for its assigned function; dance exercises and routines are repeated until the response to a given stimulus becomes automatic. This mode emphasizes speed, precision, and invariability, and unnecessary strain is avoided because it wears down the parts. Consequently, all stresses introduced in the training program are within carefully controlled (and possibly scientifically established) limits. The body-as-machine notion lends itself to a somewhat cold or neutral instructional mode, as machines, lacking sentience, respond to neither encouragement nor blame. In this mode the dance teacher is really a technician/ programmer who structures, controls, and monitors activities. He or she puts the machines through their paces, touching on all the functions the machines are expected to perform and ensuring that individual execution measures up to the quantitatively established standard.

This instructional mode is used both in sports and dance, although the tradition-bound dance world is much slower to incorporate scientific findings. Body-as-machine training is useful for dance activities in which the performer is not likely to have to cope with changing conditions (as in folk dance but not improvisation), in which the precision of form is rigidly prescribed

Figure 4.6. Body as machine. *Note.* Illustration courtesy of J. Allan Wellman.

(as in ballet), and activities in which a basic movement skill is repeated again and again (as in chorus lines). However, this metaphor's lack of flexibility is its major liability. The machine efficiently does what it is designed to do, but it cannot change what it does. A well-schooled ballerina often has difficulty with modern dance, and a ballroom dancer seldom performs abstract expressionistic dances. The body-as-machine notion also leads one to think of the body as a collection of parts connected by mechanical chains of cause and effect. This concept interferes with the dancer's experience of body as an organic whole, and can also lead the teacher to concentrate on a single offending body part and overlook the potential repercussions for the entire body. Finally, the metaphor leads to a disregard for motivational and psychological factors in students, creating for the students a schism between his or her thinking, feeling, struggling self and the machines of physically expert bodies. Training in this mode has less to do with breaking a beastly will and indolent habit than with adjustment and tuning of a precision machine. As with any technological enterprise, the side effects of technology receive little consideration, even though they can be devastating in terms of the long-range damages to the human beings involved.

The Body as Objet d'Art

In this metaphor the body is regarded as an artistic object, a thing of beauty (see Figure 4.7). This beauty is measured by a standardized image or form established by each culture and epoch. Each person compares him- or herself with this standard and endeavors to match it, as with the sculptured body builder or the willowy ballerina. Standards of beautiful movement also exist, again tacitly set by a given culture at a given time. These standards create an aesthetic movement vocabulary; motions are selected for their inherent loveliness from the range of what the human body can perform. The individual then works to acquire this vocabulary so as to present his or her body in the most impressive light. This body metaphor also includes the opposite; just as there are standards for beauty, there are also criteria for that which is grotesque. Within these standards, factors such as social status and prestige undoubtably encourage inter- or intracultural adaptations.

The most common instructional perspective in dance education that springs from this body metaphor places heavy emphasis on the visual dimension of the dance experience. Dancers diet stringently to put on or take off weight or undertake special exercises to slim or build up certain areas of the body. In terms of dance movement, emphasis is placed on the relatively static aspects of action, such as *placement*, or posture, and *line*, or posing and positioning. Transformation is a corollary of this metaphor—the student struggles to transform from an ugly duckling into a swan. In order to transform students, the teacher must represent the ideal that the students want to embody. Accordingly, the mode of instruction is heavily iconic (Bruner, 1966), including demonstration by the teacher and imitation by the students, usually aided by

Figure 4.7.   Body as objet d'art. *Note.*   Illustration courtesy of J. Allan Wellman.

mirrors in which students can watch themselves. In addition, the teacher stands ready to correct mistakes in form made by the students and may actually touch or mold the student's body to achieve the desired configuration. In Bali, as an extreme example, experienced dancers stand behind their young female dance students and actually manipulate the girls' limbs in the prescribed patterns of classical Balinese dance.

The classical ideal of beauty in Western movement tradition was born in the royal courts of post-Renaissance Europe, and we still mimic the rigidly erect posture and turned out stance of the courtier. When the purpose of dance training is to acquire the physical attributes of the aristocracy of beauty and to arrange the body attractively so as to make the most graceful and impressive exhibition of the self, the body-as-object-beautiful approach is remarkably successful, especially when the student is blessed with long legs, slender physique, flexible joints, and the like. In fact, schools that adhere to this body metaphor often reject students whose body proportions are considered substandard. Instruction based on this metaphor is limited by its inclination to overemphasize visual perception at the expense of kinesthetic sensation. This perpetuates a perception of movement as a series of positions. Often the flow and dynamic rhythm of a movement phrase is lost to the student who has been too strongly indoctrinated in the body-as-object-beautiful notion. Moreover, this metaphor supports self-conscious posing, which can lead to a kind of narcissism. We are socialized to affirm our own and other's premises about our characters, and we accomplish this via visual feedback that in turn supports a limited self-concept.

The Body as Child

The fourth metaphor is Rousseauistic in that the body is thought of as a noble savage or gifted innocent (see Figure 4.8). In this view the body is seen as pure and natural, with emphasis on the active, inquiring, and creative. As with a child, the hunger for experience is seen in a positive light, and the orientation is developmental. The instructional implication stemming from this metaphor (as used, for example, in dance improvisation) is that less is more; the teacher provides opportunities for experience and lets the body find its own way and make its own sense of what happens. With this mode, instructors use emulation of movement sequences, open-ended movement problems in which several creative solutions are viable, and movement games that promote spontaneity.

Instruction based on the body-as-child metaphor is useful in dance education that strives to induce creativity, variability of response, and easy coordination.

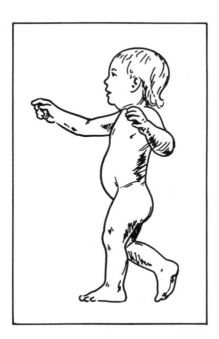

Figure 4.8. Body as child. *Note.* Illustration courtesy of J. Allan Wellman.

Unlike others, this metaphor approaches the body respectfully, but not restrictively. Consequently, students learn to listen to their own kinesthetic stirrings and to value them as a source of knowledge. This facilitates experiencing the self as an organic whole engaged in a constantly evolving dialectic. The body-as-child metaphor, however, usually does not lead to the development of high level dance skills or virtuosity. It also tends to produce a kind of conceit in which students and teachers, like babies delightedly wiggling their toes, become entranced with their own insights and relatively slight accomplishments. Finally, the notion of body as child may lead the student to be overprotective of his or her body and to avoid challenging physical tasks that would lead to mastery and greater physical maturity. The role of the teacher within this metaphor is complex. A carefully planned curriculum must underlie the open-endedness of the dance activities, while clearly delineated movement concepts and skills should lead to kinesthetic experiences.

Carol Lynne Moore has shown that each body metaphor has both favorable and unfavorable implications for dance instruction. Almost every dancer has experienced each instructional model and in this sense may be compared to a *chimera*, a mythological creature composed of the parts of several different animals. Only as we elucidate the shadowy, phantom creatures of past experience that inhabit our minds will we know better the nature of ourselves. Serious dance teachers must not only look deeply into themselves to see what metaphor they tacitly employ but must also question what lies in students' minds, as teacher expectations are reflected in students' attitudes and efforts.

We now turn from a dance instructional perspective based on metaphoric images to a widely-used method of dance instruction that is based on *polarities* or extremes of movement expression.

Polar Perspective

Barbara Mettler, a dance teacher and creative movement pioneer, is the most widely known practitioner of this mode of dance instruction. Her book, *Materials of Dance as a Creative Art Activity* (1979), is used as the source document for the following discussion. Intrinsic to Barbara Mettler's teaching methodology is her philosophy of dance. A staunch believer in dance as art, Mettler (1980) states, "In its purest and most basic form, dance is art, the art of body movement" (p. 1). Mettler (1980) believes movement is the material of the art of dance, and says, "Movement has physical properties with which the dancer can work as objectively as the sculptor works with clay" (p. 9). This objectivity in presenting her world view of dance as art is the basis of her polar dance instructional mode. Ultimately, she believes that the art resides in and emanates from the forms of movement. "It is the movement forms, not the body itself, which are the substance of the art" (Mettler, 1980, p. 9). From this perspective we will take a closer look at Barbara Mettler's polar perspective.

Progressions

The dance instruction materials for this mode are presented progressively, systematically, and predictably. Strict gradations are followed, such as from simple movements to complex ones, from individual movement studies to large group dances, from single body parts to combinations of parts, and from very restrictive movement problems to nonrestrictive ones. A sense of polarity becomes apparent as these progressions are applied to actual dance teaching sessions. For example, the progression from individual movement study to large group dance begins with students individually solving the same problem, such as "How many ways can your head move?" Next, the students work in pairs, trios, or quartets to solve the problem, which becomes more complex as more people join the group. Finally, large groups are formed to work on the problem. Examples of this exercise are, "Create a group dance with a heads-only theme" or, "Using hands-only contact with each other, compose a group dance illustrating the range of head movements." Students perform their dances for other students, and all students observe each other with as much intensity as they move themselves. The creative act pervades the entire teaching/learning/observing process.

Poles of Movement Expression

Within the progressions are the basic movement material problems, which are usually stated and presented as extremes. Each movement element has an individual continuum or range of experience. At each end of the continuum is an extreme state, thus students must resolve two movement problems in order to sense the full extent of the element. To illustrate, we consider the element of force (or energy), whose poles are tension and relaxation. The student must express these extremes with the challenge of producing no movement at either pole (i.e., extreme tension results in rigidity while extreme relaxation results in inertness or flaccidity). The student is also asked to experience gradual tension and relaxation, sudden tension and relaxation, and combinations such as sudden tension and gradual relaxation. These individual movement experiences are developed further in duets, small groups, and large groups. The ultimate objective is to introduce students to the full range of dynamic movement through learning to experience the extremes of tension and relaxation, as Mettler (1979) explains, "All body movement is characterized by alternation and balance of tension and relaxation" (p. 122).

Some of Mettler's many other movement and sensation poles are listed below:

Force

strong—weak
forceful—forceless
active—passive
explosive—sustained

Space

large—small
curved—straight
high—low
center—periphery
forwards—backwards

Time

slow—fast
regular—irregular
long duration—short duration
accelerated—decelerated

Organic Growth

Barbara Mettler's instructional mode is integrated with and reflects her notion of an organic class, from which themes of progression and polarity emerge. The concept is best described in her own words (Mettler, 1979):

> If each class is a creative experience for the teacher, no two classes will be alike. The teacher will improvise freely with the material as he prepares the class, just as the students improvise with it when it is given to them.

> The form of each class will be an organic growth, one creative problem growing out of another to meet the needs of a particular group at a particular time. Each class will grow out of the preceding one in accordance with the student's development from lesson to lesson.

> Every class should be a satisfying experience in itself—it should never be approached merely as some future satisfying experience.

> A class should be like a dance, having continuity from beginning to end, clarity of form, variety of material, theme development, balance of ac-

tivity and rest, and all the other factors which make up a complete dance experience.

The success of a class as a complete dance experience depends on the creative skill of the teacher and on the receptivity of the students. . . . Just as the student is expected to solve creatively the problem given him by the teacher, the teacher must solve creatively the problems which are given to him by the class. (p. 417)[1]

Conclusions

This chapter demonstrates that dance material can be presented in a variety of ways. The teacher's world view clearly influences her or his instructional climate and methodology and is not lost on students, who historically have been drawn to teachers who demonstrate singular styles and attitudes towards the teaching and learning of dance. We now take a closer look at the learners themselves, as it is critical to understand how and under what conditions their learning takes place. Chapter 5 discusses dance learning, giving special emphasis to learning theories for dance.

Key Terms

Academic learning time—actual time devoted to school or curricular learning

Appropriate behavior—compatible, fitting behavior

Body metaphors—objects substituted for the human body to suggest certain parallels

Chimera—an imaginary person or animal comprised of incongruous parts

Command—to direct or order

Counteractive—giving no direction or leadership, resulting in opposition and anarchy

Duration—the time during which a behavior, action, or event lasts

Episodic—made up of loosely connected behaviors, actions, or events

Inappropriate behavior—unsuitable, incompatible behavior

Incidence—rate of occurrence or influence

Interactive—giving opportunities and directions for actions with and between groups

Inventive—giving suggestions and allowing for creativity and improvisation

---

[1]From *Materials of Dance as a Creative Art Activity* (p. 417) by B. Mettler, 1979, Tucson, AZ: Mettler Studios. Copyright 1979 by Barbara Mettler Hammer. Reprinted by permission.

Learning—knowledge, skill, or understanding acquired through instruction or study

Metaphoric—suggesting a likeness by substituting one idea or object for another

Neutral behavior—behavior characterized by disinterest or disengagement

Off-task behavior—behavior unrelated to the task at hand

Plexyn—a complex software program that encodes, times, transcribes, and analyzes behavioral data

Polar—diametrically opposite

Progression—continued and connected series; a sequence

Quantitative—involving the measurement of quantity or amount

Relaxation—absence of or relief from tension, anxiety, or strain

Tension—mental, physical, or emotional stress or tightness

Time on task—actual time spent actively pursuing an assigned learning task

Weltanschauung—a comprehensive world view from a specific or personal standpoint

Student Activities and Assignments

1. Identify the instructional situations of several dance teachers. Invent your own names for situations that are not represented in this chapter's discussion.
2. Add body metaphors from your own experience to Carol Lynne Moore's list. Describe each metaphor fully, and substantiate your description with several examples.
3. Explain your advice to teachers who fall into the brick wall quadrant and the babysitting quadrant of Gray's quantitative model of dance teaching and learning.
4. Obtain a copy of Barbara Mettler's *Materials of Dance as a Creative Art Activity*, and teach one of her progressions or lessons to a class. Evaluate your own response and the students' responses to this instructional mode.

Further Reading

Ritson, R.J. (1987). Psychomotor skill teaching: Beyond the command style. *Journal of Physical Education, Recreation and Dance,* **58**(6), 36-37.

Sandback, P.R. (1986). Structuring beginning choreographic experiences: A method to ensure success. *Journal of Physical Education, Recreation and Dance*, **57**(9), 38-40.

Shute, S., Dodds, P., Placek, J., Rife, F., & Silverman, S. (1982). Academic learning time in elementary school movement education: A descriptive analytic study. *Journal of Teaching in Physical Education*, **1**(2), 3-14.

Chapter 5
Dance Learning

Chapters 3 and 4 were devoted to dance teaching and dance teachers, whose roles and responsibilities are defined by their students. This chapter discusses the student's role in the teaching/learning process.

Learning opportunities are inherent in the whole range of dance activities, and learning will occur throughout the dance curriculum whether such assumptions are explicit or not. This chapter addresses the critical role of dance learning in the dance education process. Dance learning should not be confused with learning through dance, that is, dance-aided learning or learning other subjects via the dance medium, a popular rationale used in the 1970s to justify dance's place in the curriculum. This chapter does not attempt to apply every aspect of learning to dance education or the art of dance. There are three main reasons for this; first, learning is too complex an operation to be closely analyzed in any discipline; second, learning is an evolving concept whose axioms tend to change with changing technologies and points of view; and third, insufficient dance research exists in the area of learning theory to warrant a unique theory of dance learning. Thus, selected aspects of learning theory for dance are presented, culminating in a model for dance learning based on the latest expert systems information. The first discussion focuses on how dancers learn, followed by some dance-based definitions of learning. Next, the forms of dance learning and the factors that affect dance learning are presented to portray dance as a pedagogical entity in and of itself. The section of learning theories offers a summary of old order theories plus a description of new order thinking and speculation based on Alvin Toffler's futuristic conclusions. Finally, dance learning is presented as information processing, and expert systems research is used to describe a tentative dance learning model.

How Dancers Learn

Strategies

Dancers come to class with certain notions about how to learn. Both beginning and experienced dancers ultimately discover the ways most comfortable for them to learn to dance. Ellen Jacob (1981), a professional dancer, calls these individual methods "tricks," and summarizes them as follows: "Some people need words and analysis in order to absorb new movement, while others seem to soak it up like a sponge, without any conscious reference points. Some dancers get the general shape, direction and feeling of the movement first and fill in the details later; many find rhythm the key. Some start by learning the beginning and end of a phrase, others concentrate on the transitions or joining steps" (p. 203).

When children are taught to dance, their learning behaviors are less sophisticated yet more apparent. Mary Joyce (1984), children's dance teacher in San Mateo, California, surveyed the children in her classes and asked them to describe how they learned to dance. She found that children before the age of 10 tend to copy and to learn activities that they think are "fun." She also found that children learn feelings as well as actions and have difficulty separating the two. They learn dance by imitation first and then later by recognizing the muscular states and body alignments. Joyce also asked the children what helped them to learn, and she summarized their responses as follows:

1. *Manipulation*—They liked the teacher to actually move their bodies into a correct shape and, by touching, help them do a movement correctly.
2. *Working until they feel it*—They liked working a muscle until they actually felt it.

3. *Use of mirror, floor, or object*—They felt they improved when they saw how they looked in a mirror, or when the floor or some object was used (such as feeling their backs against the floor or picking up socks with their toes).
4. *Demonstration*—They liked to be shown, not told, how to do a movement. They wanted to see it first.
5. *Imagery*—They liked teachers who used word pictures.

Learning by doing

People learn most effectively by doing. Fortunately, in dance all learning is manifested by actions even when it is stimulated or initiated by words, images, sounds, or textures. Dance can be considered the complete learning process, a contention on which William James (1983) elaborates in a physiological context: "An impression which simply flows in at the pupil's eyes and ears and in no way modifies his acting life is an impression gone to waste. It is physiologically incomplete" (p. 7).

Other dance theorists believe that to learn about learning dance, one must participate in it (and thereby affect it). Susan Stinson (1985) believes that the goal of education in dance is to stimulate more learning:

The most essential questions in children's dance, I think, are not related to how we can get children to learn . . . but what we want them to know and do. When such questions become primary, we are trainers of children, not educators. Our goal is not to shape behavior, but to ignite the children's capacity to create their own knowledge . . . in the context of the knowledge of others. (p. 223)

Like Joyce, Stinson contends that dance teachers need to ask students what dancing feels like, what it means to them, and what works and what doesn't. Stinson says, "We need to find out what they are learning besides the things we think we are teaching" (p. 235).

Learning by Expressing

Others who write about dance learning stress the expressiveness of dance learning and believe that children's natural integration between feeling and movement should be revived, if not relearned, by adults. "Perhaps what is most important," states Toby Hankin (1986), dance teacher at the University of Colorado, "particularly as we introduce beginners to the art of dance, is that they experience movement as an expressive activity, one that is intimately tied to human feeling." (p. 37). She strongly maintains that beginning with early dance instruction equal attention should be given to dance's expressive content and its movement content. Indeed, people who do not learn to dance expressively will not be able to perform, not because they cannot run, leap, balance, or pirouette, but because they will have nothing to communicate.

Ultimately, dance learning is a search for meaning. Dance learning is enhanced when students gain meaning and generate meaningful relationships kinesthetically and cognitively. Further, says Hankin, "What students discover for themselves is most meaningfully learned" (p. 37). This axiom applies to almost everything that is learned, as discovery implies changes in attitude, values, behavior, and perception, changes that cause us to adapt, layer, or dismantle our knowledge base. Common axioms of learning are best understood by taking a closer look at definitions of learning.

Views of Learning

Most psychology books (and very few dance education books) devote considerable discussion to learning behavior. The perspectives from which education researchers look at learning are the cornerstones of their theories and applications. Some of these views are reproduced here to illustrate their range and diversity and their possible usefulness to dance learning.

Behavior Modification

Learning can be simply defined as the modification of perception and behavior. A dance student learns to skip after she modifies (through practice) the way she sequences steps and hops. Her perception of locomotion changes, too, and she also expands her range of movement, or her possibilities of adaptive behavior. Based on this example, McGeouch and Irion (1952) define learning as "change in performance through conditions of activity, practice, and experience" (p. 5).

Environment

Inherent in the definitions given thus far is the assumption that something or someone has ignited or initiated the learning process, that some sensory input or stimulation has occurred. In fact, learning is dependent on such stimulation and cannot happen in its absence. Thus, says Bernard (1965), "learning depends on the inclination and ability to receive and respond to stimulation from the environment" (p. 5). Environment is critical to dance learning and is addressed in more detail in a later section.

Physical Bases

Physical attributes of the learner may be inherited (i.e., genetically programmed), congenital, or developed during the growing process. Learning and movement, for example, are inseparably integrated in the early stage of development and account for how and what is learned in childhood. The physical origins of learning influence the nature and speed of learning (Bernard, 1965).

Holism

Learning disabled students can learn in nonthreatening, success-oriented, creative movement environments, thus suggesting that learning is more holistically oriented than traditionally acknowledged. A final definition of learning takes this into consideration. Clearly, the integration of quantitative (analytic and computational) and qualitative (intuitive and heuristic) processing of stimuli ensures the full use of human potential. This integration can be called holistic, as it lends itself to the view that reality is made up of organic or unified wholes that are greater than the sum of their parts. In other words, learning is a matrix. Movement therapist and former professional dancer Kate Witkin (1977) writes, "No single aspect of the learning process can be extracted from its complex, web-like surroundings" (p. 33). Holistic learning, the integration of cognitive, perceptual, and motor processes that enable one to function optimally in the environment, is the most desirable kind of learning.

What Dancers Learn

Dance learning, whether behavioral, physical, environmental, or holistic, can take several forms (e.g., learning to perform, learning to participate, learning to create, learning to appreciate, learning to compose or choreograph, and learning to be dance literate). Harold Bernard, in his book *Psychology of Learning and Teaching* (1965), lists six forms of learning that readily apply to dance:

1. *Sensorimotor skills*—skills performed automatically, such as walking, running, sitting, and falling. These actions become so automatic that they can occur simultaneously with other actions. The stimulus for these movements comes automatically from muscles and joints. All physically able persons learn these skills without intensive or specific training.
2. *Perceptual motor skills*—drilled skills, such as ballet exercises, ballroom dance steps, and jazz dance routines. These skills differ from sensorimotor skills in that they are linked to the dancer's intellect. They are typically voluntary, observable, and purposeful. Learning these skills depends on information received from the environment, such as instructions, demonstrations, and manipulation of body parts. The learner's perception of this information is equally important and directly influences the skill learning.
3. *Perceptual learning*—pattern recognition and analogy formation such as folk dances, children's dances, and ethnic dances. Dancers with some experience can readily see familiar patterns or recognize steps in newly presented dance material. The stimulus for this form of learning arises from previous experience and conditioning.
4. *Associational learning*—movement connotations such as ideokinetics, imagery, and drama. The associations attached to movements are better known as meanings, and the stimuli for learning involve providing rich

associations. The power of the dance movements can recall feelings, states, scenes, and even objects. Conversely, certain verbal images can connote distinct movements, phrases, or entire dances.

5. *Conceptual learning*—abstracts and concepts such as dance expressionism, minimal dance, and thematic dance. Concepts involve interrelationships and complex cogency (e.g., motherhood). Conceptual learning depends on a certain level of maturity and is constantly evolving through experiences at home, in school, at work, and through community and society.

6. *Problem solving*—creative responses such as in structured improvisation and creative dramatics. In dance, this is considered the most valuable form of learning, as the responses are dependent on the dance student's ability to perceive the problem, manipulate abstract ideas, draw on previous learnings, analyze and synthesize possible solutions, and test and evaluate the solution. Problem solving is considered in more detail later in this chapter.

Perceptual and behavioral changes involved in learning may be manifested in many other ways, some of which are listed as follows:

- Discrimination
- Incidental
- Neurophysiological
- Nonverbal
- Observational
- Sequential
- Social
- Spatial
- Team
- Trial and error
- Rhythmic
- Values

Regardless of what form learning takes, a receptive mind and a willing body are the most important requirements for dance learning. Ellen Jacob (1981) suggests: "Open your intuitive antennae and trust that learning goes on at many levels. Don't worry if you don't always know intellectually what your body is doing. Often the body understands before the mind does" (p. 204). All forms of dance learning, moreover, are affected by a variety of conditions which are subsumed by three major factors—input, attention, and motivation.

Factors Affecting Dance Learning

Much of what follows is an adaption of Evelyn Schurr's discussion on the variables that inhibit or enhance the learning of skills (Schurr, 1980). It is appropriate and applicable to the learning of skills and concepts, and the understanding of dance.

Sensory Input

The dance student receives the material to be learned through the sensory organs of the body. Students have varying degrees of sensory capacities that determine the amount and quality of stimuli that will be received. Once received, the sensory stimuli is interpreted, or perceived. The dance student's perception is affected by earlier experiences, reasons for learning, interest in the material, and the teaching methods. In dance learning, the students' familiarity with the teacher's way of moving affects how readily they learn new steps and sequences.

Attention

Paying attention to the amount and quality of stimuli is critical to learning and is a responsibility of both the learner and the teacher. For optimal learning, the movement space should be free of distractions (such as noise and traffic) and physical obstacles. Too much or too little information can reduce a student's attention, and certain kinds of information (e.g., irrelevant or repetitive) can affect the span of attention. Other participants can also distract a student. "Sometimes it's hard to resist wanting to look like someone else, particularly because one learns to dance chiefly by imitating others," states Ellen Jacob (1981). She tells dance students, "Expect some movements to register very differently on you than on your teacher or classmates, and remember that this is what makes you unique as a dancer" (p. 204). Contrastingly, in group improvisation (particularly contact improvisation) and creative problem-solving dance situations the movements of others serve as stimuli and should be observed.

Motivation

Motivation is the relative energy that directs behavior toward certain goals. It refers to the internal conditions that arouse, sustain, and direct behavior in response to the learning environment. Hence the teacher does not actually motivate the student; however, the teacher can manipulate environmental factors that increase or decrease motivation, some of which are discussed next.

Arousal level. Arousal levels are specific to the individual student and to the task to be learned, and they are tied to the student's emotional state. Arousal can be measured by both emotional and muscular tension. Thus, too much or too little tension will adversely affect the motivation to learn. In a dance class, performance anxiety frequently creates inhibitions and mistakes, and for this reason nonthreatening environments are suggested for dance classes that involve children, boys, and beginners.

Interest level.   Dance students learn best and most quickly when they have a purpose and interest in what they are learning. Individualizing learning and personal responsibility for learning usually increase students' interest in dancing and make dancing more meaningful. High interest levels support motivation and can be maintained by teacher enthusiasm and by the introduction of new and challenging material.

Goal orientation.   Dance students should know the goal toward which they are working. If they participate in setting the goal, they are more apt to understand it and be more motivated to achieve it. Mary Joyce (1984) advises, "Be direct . . . tell the children the goal of the technique you want to teach them. Draw from them or show them how to do it. Have them use that technique, making it part of their knowledge and skill" (p. 10). Stating goals gives dance students a clear picture of the teacher's expectations; this in turn sustains motivation.

Transfer of Skills

Efficiency in and ease of learning new dance skills depend on the student's ability to apply previous learning to the new task. Transfer of skills is motivational but not automatic. A knowledge base of movement fundamentals is desirable, if not essential, for learning new dance skills. Many dance programs require a course of movement fundamentals to facilitate the transfer of learning. Elizabeth Hayes devotes a significant portion of her book, *An Introduction to the Teaching of Dance* (1964), to movement fundamentals as preparation for dance. She cautions readers not to confuse these preparatory techniques with dance, as the techniques are "the means to an end and that end is dancing" (p. 17). The concept of learning to learn, which is important in increasing the ability to master new and numerous dance skills, is seen as an ideal motivational aid to transference.

Practice

Too often a new skill or concept is introduced in dance classes, then new tasks are added with little opportunity for practice and mastery. This leads to a decline in the motivation to learn and subsequently to little actual learning. Also, excessive practice of a dance skill can lead to boredom, thwarting motivation to learn. Dance teachers sometimes attempt to teach too much in a given amount of time, thus failing to help students learn and retain skills and concepts. Teachers must schedule practice and rehearsal opportunities to promote optimum learning, continued motivation, and a sense of self-satisfaction.

Feedback

Feedback is one of the most important factors affecting learning. Feedback is highly motivational and involves more than simply the knowledge of results.

In dance, it involves the detection and correction of errors, errors that may be as obvious as poor alignment or as subtle as intimate facial expression. Feedback can actively augment dance learning by consolidating what has been learned. Thus, feedback has three functions:

1. Motivation
2. Change or correction of immediate performance
3. Reinforcement of learning

Feedback can be received internally (kinesthetically) or externally (verbally and nonverbally). Use of the videocamera in dance classes provides students with instant and effective external feedback and is particularly valuable when dance students are rehearsing or choreographing.

Readiness to Learn

Readiness to learn dance is most usually based on maturity of dance students. Physical maturity isn't always related to age; it includes strength, endurance, fitness, coordination, and rhythmic acuity. Intellectual and social maturity must also be consistent with the level of dance activities. Motivation to learn dance is greatly enhanced when the readiness level is appropriate.

Retention

The retention of dances and routines is directly related to practice and over-learning. Practice should simulate an actual performance situation as much as possible. Overlearning is practice that is continued after the dance is well learned. Both practice and overlearning are motivational and give the dance student a sense of accomplishment and success, encouraging the student to learn more.

Learning Theories

Many theories of learning exist, from traditional theories to more recent *new order theories*. New order theories include neurological theories, information processing theories, and systems theories (e.g., expert systems and knowledge management systems); cognitive scientists and artificial intelligence researchers lead the research in these areas. A brief overview of the traditional theories is presented next, followed by a detailed account of one of the new order theories—learning as information processing.

Theories of learning, according to educational psychologist John De Cecco (1968), describe and explain the conditions under which learning does and does not take place. A theory of learning, he adds, applies to all organisms, learning tasks, and situations in which learning may occur. It explains, predicts, and controls the way environmental conditions affect the learning of the organism. Moreover, a theory of learning is much broader and more basic than a theory of teaching. No single theory of learning exists; some are narrow and domain-specific, while others are broad and far-reaching. The narrow theories of learning are typically developed in the laboratory and are quite precise, while broad theories deal with everyday situations and are more generalized and flexible. De Cecco believes that the narrow theories have the greater rigor, the broader theories the greater relevance. Jan Hyatt's holistic learning theory for dance constitutes a broad theory. She believes that children think and learn in multiple ways. Holistic learning, she says, is an integration of thinking, feeling, and movement energies that covers the full human potential spectrum. Dance learning, says Hyatt (1985), is a "holistic activity accomplished through the interweaving of physicality, sensibility, and intelligence for the purpose of body control" (p. 41).

For much of this century and until very recently, learning theories have been dominated by a number of general, powerful ideas. The development of computer technology and information science has somewhat overshadowed these ideas, yet while they are no longer in force, these older learning theories still influence educational practices and curriculum design. Dance education is affected by these traditional theories chiefly because a replacement set of learning theories has not yet emerged. Following is an overview of the traditional theories.

Early learning theories embodied attempts to link outwardly observable stimuli with outwardly observable learner responses. Learning was determined by whether the organism changed under the influence of the stimuli or remained unaffected. This stimulus-response, or *mechanistic*, explanation of learning was characteristic of the old order of learning theories. The theories were limited by the laboratory technology at the time and by the prevalent narrow, nonholistic definition of learning. Early learning theorists reconstructed the behavior of humans and animals as if they were machines, hence the term mechanistic. This metaphor was appropriate and efficient at the time, as society was comfortably settled into the industrial age and learning research was conducted within the machine-oriented environment of sterile laboratories.

Experimentation in these laboratories substantiated the limited, though widely held, view that learning involves two processes—classical and instrumental conditioning. According to British psychologists Borger and Seaborne (1982), classical conditioning involves a more basic and older form of learning and accounts for "anticipation behaviors and predetermined responses" (pp. 81-82). Borger and Seaborne wrote that instrumental conditioning "allows a more finely-tuned adaption to the environment" (pp. 81-82), inferring that this means of learning increases in importance with increasing cerebral development. These psychologists formed their learning theories largely from the study of laboratory animals—birds, dogs, and occasionally primates; the practical value of these learning theories for humans has never been fully explored.

Researchers now consider classical and instrumental conditioning theories as elementary learning methods that no longer provide adequate explanations for all learning. Field theories are still popular, and pave the way for the new order learning theories, which are addressed next.

Information Processing

Problem solving is a method of learning that dominates the creative learning aspects of dance education. Cognitive psychologists, modern learning theorists, and artificial intelligence researchers believe that problem solving (and other mental processes as well) can be rationalized and understood as information processing. Researchers have moved away from quantitative models of learning behavior (how well people perform) toward qualitative descriptions of how people think and move. This information processing model consists of three major subsystems, each containing memories (where information is stored) and processors (where information is processed; see Figure 5.1). The subsystems are as follows:

1. *Perceptual system*—Stimuli enter through the human sensors, such as the eyes, ears, muscles, and skin. The perceptual system consists of these sensors plus holding memories called *buffer* memories, which briefly store the incoming information (or percepts) while awaiting processing (Harmon and King, 1985).
2. *Cognitive system*—As the sensors constantly place vast amounts of information into their buffer memories, the cognitive system proceeds to organize the information. The cognitive processor does this with a selective encoding process by which the perceptual information is selected and transferred to working memory. Educators refer to this as "paying attention" or being "on-task." For the simplest of movement tasks, these percepts are transferred directly to the motor subsystem. For example, in dance education such moves as jumps, pliés, rolls, and arm circles, which are habitual and require little coordination or thought, transfer directly. More complex dance moves involve more information and therefore more processing.
3. *Motor system*—After the information is transferred to the motor system, appropriate actions are initiated. The motor processors implement muscle activity, which results in observable dance movements and postures.

Problem Solving

Problem solving is a subcategory of information processing. Harmon and King (1985) define problem solving as "the process of starting in an initial state and searching through a problem space in order to identify the sequence of

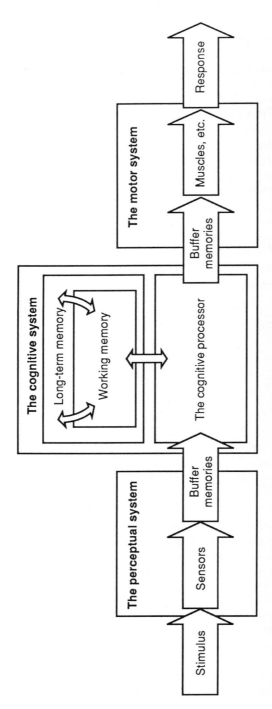

Figure 5.1. The human information processing system. *Note.* From *Expert Systems* (p. 23) by P. Harmon and D. King, 1985, New York: Wiley. Copyright 1985 by John Wiley and Sons, Inc. Adapted by permission.

operations or actions that will lead to a desired goal" (p. 27). Searching is the key to problem solving. Lois Ellfeldt, throughout *A Primer for Choreographers* (1967), stresses this relentless search for new ideas, resources, and options in the process of creating dance forms. The problem space is where all options reside and can be bound (as in dance reconstructions) or unbound (as in improvisation). Dance students, both beginning and experienced, can solve complex movement problems because they have stored many experiences that can be used to simplify the problem. Large problem spaces can be reduced to more manageable ones by using knowledge from past experiences. Experienced or professional choreographers (and many dancers, too) have accumulated sufficiently diverse and meaningful knowledge about dance to swiftly and efficiently prune the search space presented by the problem and develop satisfying or workable solutions.

Dance Knowledge Base

Compiled dance knowledge is that base of skills and understandings that is accessible and primed for problem solving (see Figure 5.2). Learning, or building this knowledge base, occurs formally and informally (heuristically). The formal study of dance, which typically includes lectures, textbooks, term papers, lecture demonstrations, and films, may increase the knowledge base about dance, but it is useless unless the student knows how to apply it. The informal learning of dance is experience based. Dance knowledge compiled from experience results in heuristics—discoveries resulting from selective searching. According to Harmon and King (1985), "Heuristics are rules-of-thumb that prune search space to a manageable size. They try to focus attention on a few key patterns" (p. 31).

Heuristic researchers believe that performers can improve by organizing and sorting heuristic knowledge much the same way they do formal knowledge. According to Harmon and King, "Compiled heuristic knowledge, that is experience that is well-organized and indexed, in long term memory, gives us the edge when we face and solve numerous problems" (p. 31).

Dance Training Versus Dance Education

This information processing model for dance involves the distinction between knowledge compiled from experience and knowledge compiled from school study. Dance students use knowledge from teachers and books to develop abstract theories that can be applied to a large number of different dance situations, but rarely provide specific direction in a particular situation. However, experience in problem solving teaches dance students heuristics or *domain dependent facts* that students gradually compile into *domain theories* that tell them how to perform in a specific situation. Harmon and King (1985) refer to domain dependent knowledge as surface knowledge and call knowledge gained from books deep knowledge (see Figure 5.3).

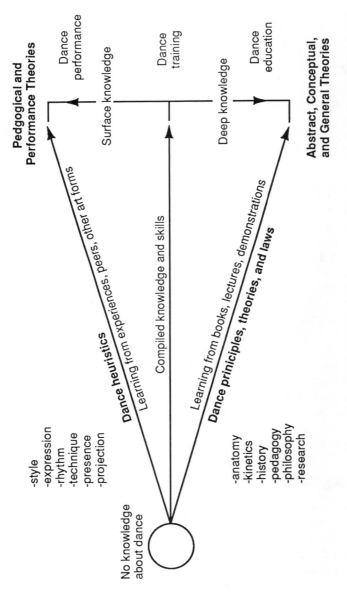

Figure 5.2. Development of a dance knowledge base. *Note.* From *Expert Systems* (p. 30) by P. Harmon and D. King, 1985, New York: Wiley. Copyright 1985 by John Wiley and Sons, Inc. Adapted by permission.

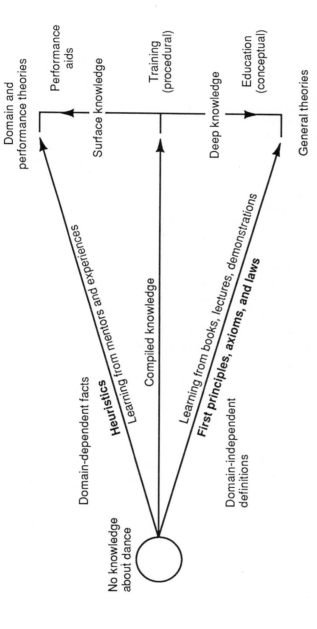

Figure 5.3. Varieties of dance knowledges and their relationships to instructional strategies. *Note.* From *Expert Systems* (p. 33) by P. Harmon and D. King, 1985, New York: Wiley. Copyright 1985 by John Wiley and Sons, Inc. Adapted by permission.

Dance educators can learn from the conclusions and ongoing research of expert systems writers. Since the 1970s, researchers working in training and instructional design for business have identified three different approaches to instruction that have bearing on dance instruction.

1. *Instructional aids*—provide minimal contact with an instructor as students are instructed via dance handbooks, do-it-yourself manuals, checklists, and videos
2. *Training*—provides some theoretical information, but only in the interest of accomplishing a special task (e.g., a certain dance technique)
3. *Education*—provides conceptual principles that will allow dance students to think in broad and abstract terms

A more rigorous distinction can be drawn between education and training if one stresses what the dance student will do with the knowledge after completing the course of instruction. Training occurs when coursework is simply applied to a specific situation or performance, for example when a student learns the polka in order to dance in a production of *Seven Brides for Seven Brothers*. Education occurs when the student learns the polka in order to prepare for the study of East European folk dances. Ultimately, the focus on dance concepts and procedures does not determine the difference between dance training and education, but rather the end objective or long-term goal of the dance learning experience is most important.

Dance training prepares the student to perform a specific technique or apply a certain knowledge to a singular dance setting. Education, say Harmon and King (1985), "teaches what it teaches more or less for its own sake" (p. 237). Dance education, then, is committed to lifelong learning and knowledge acquisition.

Conclusions

The findings of learning theory must be integrated with the knowledge base of dance—whether it is defined or undefined and whether it is composed of facts, skills, myths, understandings, concepts, or hearsay. The subsequent body of dance knowledge must in turn be structured and readied for delivery to the learners. This delivery system is referred to as curriculum construction; chapter 6 describes, analyses and rationalizes the dance curriculum.

Key Terms

Artificial intelligence—computer-generated ability to apply and manipulate knowledge

Attention—close or careful observation of or concentration on an event or object

Conditioning—the process of training to exhibit a new or modified behavioral response

Feedback—the return of information about the result of an action or process

Gestalt psychology—the study of behavior that holds that a psychological phenomenon is only the sum of its parts

Goal oriented—focused on a task or objective

Heuristics—exploratory problem-solving strategies or procedures that utilize self-education techniques to improve performance

Holism—the theory that reality is made up of organic or unified wholes that are greater that the simple sum of their parts

Motivation—the process of providing or receiving incentive

Perception—insight, intuition, or knowledge gained through any of the senses

Perceptual motor—combining the functions of the sensing and motor activities at the cerebral level

Practice—perform repeatedly in order to acquire or polish a skill

Problem solving—resolving uncertainties or difficult questions and situations

Readiness—state of preparedness, availability, or willingness to proceed

Retention—the capacity to remember

Sensorimotor—combining the functions of the sensing and motor activities at the neurological level

Sensory input—impulses that enter a system through the senses

Transfer of skills—learned skills and aptitudes that are readily conveyed to other situations or conditions

Student Activities and Assignments

1. Recall as many of your dance learning experiences as you can. List and describe them in terms of the stimulus-response theory of learning.
2. Observe several children's dance classes. Identify which activities or skills are learned most readily, and theorize why this is so.
3. Compare the heuristic knowledge base of dance education with the formal base. Provide several examples within each category.
4. Conduct your own research into the emerging cognition-based learning theories. Speculate what impact these may have on both scientific and informal investigations of dance learning.

Further Reading

H'Doubler, M. (1978). A way of thinking. In D.J. Falloon (Ed.), *Encores for dance* (pp. 12-13). Reston, VA: American Alliance for Health, Physical Education, Recreation and Dance.

Little, A. (1978). *Dance as learning*. Reston, VA: American Alliance for Health, Physical Education, Recreation and Dance.

Moore, E. (1978). Dance technique through problem-solving. In D.J. Falloon (Ed.), *Encores for dance* (p. 127). Reston, VA: American Alliance for Health, Physical Education, Recreation and Dance.

Chapter 6

Dance in the Curriculum and the Curriculum in Dance

The previous chapters on the teaching and learning of dance have implied the existence of a body of dance knowledge that has been planned by teachers and presented to students. In educational institutions, this body of knowledge is divided into topics or courses, the sum of which is referred to as the curriculum. All the courses of study offered by an educational institution are known as its curriculum, and much attention is given to the relationship of an institution's curriculum to its mission. A balance is maintained between courses that are deemed necessary and those that are deemed or elective. Dance curriculum should not be regarded as a means to accomplish the objectives of some other discipline, nor should it be subservient or inferior to a larger educational domain such as physical education or theater. Rather, dance should exist as a separate entity while simultaneously contributing to the realization of the institution's mission. Curriculum can thus be viewed from two perspectives—dance in the curriculum and the curriculum in dance. In either case, a curriculum is devised by those who are charged with ensuring viability and accountability in education. As a result, a curriculum, according to dance educator Sue Stinson (1985) "exists only as it comes through persons; it is a structure by which we as educators reveal our values . . . what we are teaching is ourselves" (p. 215).

This chapter discusses the curriculum as it pertains to dance in education. The discussion begins with compelling arguments for the inclusion of dance in an institution's curriculum. Next, dance is shown as a curricular vehicle for sustaining excellence in education. Finally, several state dance curriculum guidelines are presented for comparing merits, methodologies, innovations, and approaches.

Arts in Society

Why do the arts belong in our schools? A 7-point answer to this question is found in *Performing Together: The Arts in Education* (1985), a booklet jointly published by the John F. Kennedy Center for the Performing Arts, the Alliance for Arts Education, and the American Association of School Administrators. The booklet is designed for everyone concerned about learning, particularly those who are unsure or skeptical about the vital role the arts play in basic education. In light of current opposition to dance in school curricula, it seems appropriate to reproduce the seven reasons. They are as follows:

1. *The arts are a basic means of communication.* The arts are a form of human communication—like the words that make up language or the symbols that make up mathematics. The arts provide an important way to teach students how people interact with each other. For some students, the arts provide an outlet for thoughts, emotions, or aspirations they cannot express any other way. "If I could tell you what I mean," the famous modern dancer Isadora Duncan once said, "there would be no point in dancing."
2. *The arts help students develop their creativity and their creative talents.* Great scientists, including Albert Einstein, have historically come to realize the critical importance of fantasy. Studying the arts gives all students that gift. When they study drama, they can become someone else, if only for a few minutes. When they create a painting, they can see the world with fresh eyes. Research has shown that students who study the arts are also more likely to display originality and creativity in other subjects.
3. *Studying the arts helps students learn all other subjects as well.* Because the arts are such a basic means of communication, and because they provide such insight into the ways other people think, studying

the arts can enable students to learn other subjects as well. The Council for Basic Education includes the arts in its list of essential subjects that all students should study in school.

4. *Studying the arts is one of the best ways to understand human civilization.* The arts represent an essential part of a civilization. Because the arts directly reflect their creators, they provide direct communication with the past—and sometimes a glimpse of the future. A serious study of the arts is a part of any student's education. Anyone who hopes to understand ancient Greece, for example, should read some of the plays of Sophocles.

5. *Studying the arts helps students develop discipline.* When students begin to study any art form seriously, they learn immediately that they must work every day if they want to perfect their skill. When students see that professional artists must still undergo the rigorous discipline of daily practice before performing, they are learning a valuable lesson in self-discipline that will help them in their chosen art form—and in their daily lives. Student artists also see first hand that artists are always striving for—but never reaching—perfection. On Pablo Casals's 95th birthday, a reporter asked him why, although he was the world's greatest cellist, he still began each day's practice session with the same simple piece by Bach. Casals's reply was instructive: "Because I think I am getting better."

6. *Studying the arts in school helps prepare students for their adult lives.* Some of the students who study the arts in school may discover their lifetime career interest. Perhaps only a small percentage of aspiring actors, dancers, writers, musicians, or visual artists will ultimately earn a living as professional artists. But there are thousands of other jobs in the arts—technical fields such as lighting or costume design, management, promotion, and a host of others. In fact, the U.S. Bureau of Labor Statistics estimates that more than 1.3 million Americans earn their living as performing or visual artists, and that millions more are employed in other arts-related fields. Besides teaching some students about how to earn a living, the arts can teach all students important things about living. For example, mastering an art form can contribute to personal confidence. Whatever their vocation, millions of adults enjoy the arts during their leisure time. Some futurists predict that by the year 2000, the typical American will work only 20 to 30 hours per week. The arts provide citizens of the future with one enjoyable way to make the best possible use of this increased leisure time.

7. *Studying the arts helps students develop their artistic judgment.* From the moment we get dressed in the morning until we turn out the light at night, each of us makes a host of decisions that are affected by our own artistic judgment. What clothes shall we wear? What radio station will we listen to? Will we buy that magazine that catches our eye

on the newsstand? Which restaurant should we choose for a special dinner? And whether we realize it or not, as we make those decisions, we are acting on our own sense of design, color, texture, shape, pattern, order, movement, line, and scale. The arts have always been an integral part of everyday life.

Arts in Education: Eisner's Thesis

Elliot Eisner (1986) argues that "the arts are cognitive activities, guided by human intelligence, that make unique forms of meaning possible" (p. 57). He adds that these meanings require people to be literate in the arts and hence more expressive and receptive. His argument holds much significance for dance, as dance educators are finding that dance literacy is becoming increasingly important to dance learning and understanding as well as to performance and creativity. Eisner establishes that the arts involve cognition, because cognition is a critical process that enables the organism to become aware of the environment. Awareness in turn employs the functions of the senses. When the qualities of the environment are perceived they become part of consciousness. Eisner says to be aware of the environment requires that "two conditions must be satisfied. First, the qualities must be available for experiencing by a sentient human being. Second, the individual must be able to 'read' their presence" (pp. 58-59). When these conditions are met, concepts about the environment are formed. The senses are essential for providing information and further, without this conceptual information, image surrogates (e.g., words) have no meaning. Concepts, he maintains, are derived from the senses and are not at first linguistic. Eisner believes concept formation requires "the ability to perceive qualitative nuances in the qualitative world and to abstract their structural features for purposes of recall or imaginative manipulation" (p. 64). To emphasize this point with regard to schools, Eisner (1986) lists the following four implications for educational theory and subsequent curriculum design:

1. It is impossible to regard as cognitive any mental activity that is not itself rooted in sensory forms of life. Any conception of intelligence that omits the ordering of qualities through direct experience is neglecting a central feature of intellectual functioning. The mind operates whether one is performing a *pas de deux* or solving quadratic equations. The kind and number of opportunities a person is given to learn will significantly affect the degree to which his or her ability develops. Opportunities in the arts have lagged behind those in other areas of intellectual functioning as can be observed when looking at any school curriculum.

2. The realm of meaning has many mansions. It is not possible to represent or to know everything in one form. What this means for education is that—insofar as we in schools, colleges, and universities are interested

in providing the conditions that enable students to secure deep and diverse forms of meaning in their lives—we cannot in good conscience omit the fine arts. Insofar as we seek to develop the skills for securing such meanings, we must develop multiple forms of literacy. The task of the schools is to provide the conditions that foster the development of such literacy. Curricula should reflect the role of the arts in this endeavor.

3. Current educational policies and practices amount to a form of educational inequity. The amount of time devoted to cultivating abilities in the arts is extremely limited; hence students with abilities and interests in the arts are denied the opportunities that students in science, mathematics, or English receive. This inequity would cease if the arts were regarded as cognitive activities and essential to the formation of concepts and qualitative judgements about the environment. The educational inequity is particularly insidious when decisions are made about the allocation of school time, about the criteria used to identify gifted students, and about the aptitudes suitable for college and university study.

4. The cultivation of literacy in forms of artistic representation can significantly improve a student's ability to use propositional forms of representation. The ability to create or understand sociology, psychology, or economics depends on the ability to perceive qualitative nuances in the social world, the ability to conceptualize patterns from which to share what has been experienced, and the ability to write about them in a form that is compelling. Education in the arts cultivates sensitive perception, develops insight, fosters imagination, and places a premium on well-crafted form. These skills and dispositions are of central importance in both writing and reading. Without them, children are unlikely to write—not because they cannot spell but because they have nothing to say. The writer starts with vision and ends with words. The reader begins with these words but ends with vision.

Eisner concludes by stating that the interaction of the senses enriches meaning. The arts, he says, are not mere diversions from the important business of education, but essential resources.

A Case for Dance in the Schools

Dance is a precious commodity for our schools, a rare and untapped resource that along with the other arts promises to emerge as a vital, new thoroughfare in the search for educational excellence. Dance educators have always believed that dance is an educational force and that the right to dance exists within the school curriculum, not adjunctive to it. Elliot Eisner's case for arts in education applies aptly to dance; dance is an essential resource with all the attributes and strengths of a sensory-based cognitive discipline.

Every child's right to dance is presently interpreted in a variety of ways. Dance education in our schools typically resembles one or more of the following models:

- social culturalization—folk and square dance, ballroom, ethnic dance, mixers, and dancing games and rituals
- skill development—locomotor steps, ballet basics, turns, alignment, elevation, and combinations
- fitness—aerobics, rhythmic conditioning, and stretching exercises
- entertainment—school productions, jazz and tap dance, recitals, and theater dance

As prospective avenues toward strengthening dance education, these models are limited at best. The sense of artistic purpose and the concept of arts integration are notably lacking from these models. In schools, the concept of dance as art is either neglected or avoided, and as a result, students are offered noncreative substitutes such as aerobics and social dance and are denied the opportunity to seek excellence through aesthetic human movement. This neglect has contributed to the erosion of total educational performance that exists in today's schools.

What, then, should be the role of dance in educational performance? How can dance play a viable part in the strengthening of a nation's educational system? According to Araminta Little of the National Dance Association (Little, 1978), "Dance is the best medium for the development of creativity, independence, aesthetic sensitivity-perceiving, and understanding feelings and expressing them to self and others" (p. 40).

Dance is also an expression of strength, culture, and physical achievement, of a kind of excellence in motion. Dance in the schools can foster the urge to learn by involving the whole child in problem solving, exploratory activities, and information processing. Artists-in-the-schools programs motivate thousands of students to learn and to excel by exposing them to high-quality demonstrations by professional dancers and choreographers. These residencies are conducted by regionally and nationally known dance educators such as Shirley Ririe of Utah; by community dance companies like Madison, Wisconsin's Kanopy Dance Theatre; and by individual artists such as Rudy Perez of Los Angeles. The common denominator of these efforts is the conviction that dance is an art form to be shared by all.

Dance learning requires an educational setting complete with a competent instructor. Araminta Little (1978) cautions, "The performance of dance alone can't educate; exposure is not enough. Dance needs teachers who know dance and feel dance and can communicate" (p. 39). Dance needs knowledgeable, empathetic guides to lead, direct, and accompany the student explorers. Thus the level of dance guidance and instruction is a prime concern in designing curriculum and in determining the quality of dance in the schools. This quality (and also the quantity) of dance is judged both by society's perception of its value in the total curriculum and by its significance to lifelong learning. Those directly responsible, the dance teachers, are critical to the successful implementation of dance programs in our schools. Who are these people?

There are four major groups of dance teachers in the schools:

1. Dance education specialists with academic majors in dance education
2. Physical education majors with a minor in dance or dance education
3. Art, music, and drama teachers with a minor in dance education
4. Elementary education classroom teachers with a minor in dance or dance education

Criteria for a Dance Education Curriculum

Dance must meet certain criteria if it is to play a viable role in the revitalization of our schools and contribute to the overall excellence of the educational system.

First, the dance education program must be accessible. Students will not excel in dance if the concepts presented are obscure, the skills physically impossible, or the content incomprehensible. Nor will all students excel if the curriculum is not geared to reach all students.

Second, dance education must be purposeful. Dance educators must know whether the purpose of the program is socialization, fitness, aesthetics, or audience development. Educators should ensure the purpose complements the mission of the school.

Third, dance education must have credibility . Credibility is determined by several factors: caliber of teaching, support of the administration, responsiveness of parents, and strength of curriculum. The credibility of a dance program is also affected by its place in the curriculum. For example, a dance program that is part of the physical education curriculum may have less (or more) credibility than one affiliated with the drama program or one structured as an after-school repertory club.

Fourth, students must know what dance is and what they can achieve through dance. Dance is the pure art of body movement, the creation or reproduction of movement forms that do not necessarily serve a practical purpose yet can provide a deep sense of satisfaction and achievement. More than any other activity, dance helps students realize their own visions of excellence.

What Has to Be Done

Dance education is all too often incorporated into physical skills training such as gymnastics, theatrical productions, music, and special therapies. The result is dilution and confusion, leading one to question the prevalent belief that excellence can be best obtained through interdisciplinary methods. Excellence in dance is achieved most effectively when dance programs are independent of, rather than subservient to, other subjects. Dance must not be regarded as a "helping" course or activity. The scope of dance education warrants its independent status, and a corps of rigorously trained dance teachers is available to select, deliver, and evaluate the materials of dance movement. To guarantee independence and integrity, the dance education profession should ensure the following:

- Quality dance teacher preparation programs that focus on the artistic and expressive aspects of dance
- Continuing education programs in dance for teachers, administrators, and specialists
- Stronger partnerships between schools, teacher training programs, and the professional dance world
- Incentives to attract talented young people into dance teaching careers
- Greater parent and community awareness of the vital role of dance in schools and in society

Some communities are pursuing these recommendations. In Madison, Wisconsin, several schools work closely with the university, local arts organizations, private dance studios, and the media to promote, strengthen, and enhance the visibility of dance education programs. In San Mateo, California, the high school's performing arts departments (music, theater, and dance) collaborate with community theater to produce several major musical theater productions each year. While these and other similar efforts are encouraging, their import cannot easily be evaluated. How do we know when achievement in dance has occurred? How can we evaluate the effectiveness of a dance curriculum? How can we measure excellence in dance? The following section addresses these questions.

Evaluation of the Results

Excellence, in dance as in other human endeavors, involves achieving one's highest potential. Excellence reflects effort, talent, effective teaching, and the student's ability to assume responsibility for his or her own learning. The pride and satisfaction that accompany excellence may stem from performing cooperatively within a group, resolving a creative movement problem, composing a dance, or manipulating the kinetic elements of movement.

Dance education gains are difficult to assess as they often evolve slowly over time and are entwined in a tight relationship with body and self-image. However, students' attitudinal and physical changes indicate achievement, and some of these can be measured. In her monograph *Research III*, Buff Brennan (1982) lists a number of research studies in which dancer attitudes were successfully measured (Halstead, 1980; Moses, 1980). Studies have also evaluated physical changes in dancers by measuring aptitudes, skills, and physiological changes. Examples are Margaret Pappalardo's study of the effects of disco dancing on selected physiological parameters (Pappalardo, 1980) and Cynthia Ensign's examination and measurement of the effects of range, frequency, and duration of movement on student's rhythmic synchronization (Ensign, 1976). In addition, dance educators are trained to know when a dance movement, phrase, or composition transcends the ordinary; they are trained to recognize excellence in motion. A valid rationale exists for including the arts in education, the students are willing and able, the teachers are trained, the content is rich, and an approved curriculum is in place. Yet dance is still not sufficiently supported in the schools. The next section discusses roadblocks to support of dance education.

Problems to Address

Many problems facing dance education are shared by the entire educational system; they include mediocrity, compromise, confusion, illiteracy, technology, and motivation *(A Nation at Risk*, 1983). Dance programs often encounter these additional obstacles:

1. The public's view that dance is the prerogative of the rich, the educated, the nonathlete, the few
2. The general notion that equates excellence in dance with excellent dance technique
3. The cursory nature of dance in the schools, which in turn affects the level of achievement and serves as a self-fulfilling prophecy
4. The lack of financial support
5. The chasm between dance in schools and the professional world of dance
6. The myth that problem solving is a purely cognitive process and that movement creativity is unrelated to intellectual growth and achievement

To achieve the recommendation made in *A Nation at Risk* (1983) that the arts be part of the K-12 curriculum, these obstacles must be overcome. Dance education within a school's curriculum is not only valuable in and of itself but is a viable means toward excellence in the school system as a whole. To improve the quality of dance education, the schools must create more dance programs, employ more dance teachers, and provide students more access to dance. Fortunately, several states have designed curriculum guidelines for the performing arts and require high schools to provide at least one semester of a performing art as a graduation requirement. The final section of this chapter presents a selection of these dance curriculum guidelines; the reader can compare them for their individual merits and approaches.

Regional Dance Curriculum Guidelines: A Sample

Wisconsin

The Wisconsin guide (Wisconsin Department of Public Instruction, 1981) serves as a resource for the development of local school district dance education curriculum guides (see Figure 6.1). The document presents an ideal model for dance in education, one that emphasizes a conceptual, holistic approach rather than the imitative methods traditionally used in dance education. The schema focuses on the various conceptual aspects of dance and arranges them into a holistic and comprehensive education model that integrates cognitive, motor, and affective learning domains.

The authors of the document argue that dance should be intrinsic to the education of all students at all grade levels: "Dance educators have a commitment to teach students how to use movement as a medium of expression, to integrate the motor with the cognitive, to explore the bond between personality and movement, and to stretch the traditional boundaries of the educational processes." The goals of the curriculum, which involve the individual and society, are illustrated in Figure 6.2.

This approach is based on the notion of conceptual learning, which involves exploration, discovery, and application. Designing the curriculum involved development of the following components:

1. A conceptual framework stressing major theories in dance education
2. Basic subject matter content to be used by the learner, including skills and knowledge in the cognitive, motor, and affective domains of learning
3. Methods to evaluate effectiveness of the learning experience
4. A retrieval system to permit easy access to dance education resources
5. Planning forms for organizing learning units

Within the first component, sequential concepts are identified under nine broad generalizations: aesthetics; kinetics; self-awareness; kinesthetics; socialization; culturalization; creativity; appreciation; and elements of time, space, and energy. Five age levels are also identified:

Level I	K-2	Experiencing
Level II	3-4	Discovering
Level III	5-6	Understanding
Level IV	7-9	Knowing
Level V	10-12	Applying knowledge and skills

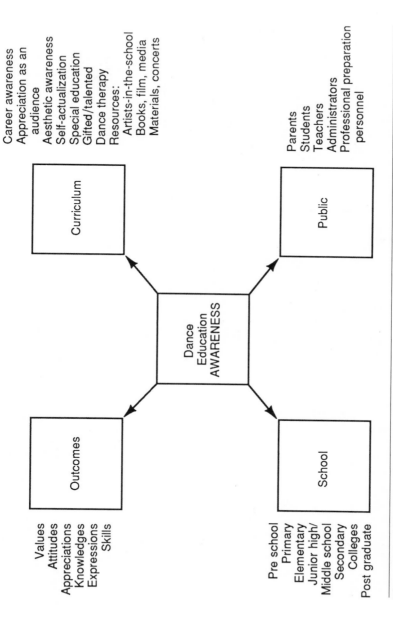

Figure 6.1. Wisconsin dance curriculum schema. *Note.* From *Dance: Creative/Rhythmic Movement Education,* Bulletin No. 2119, 1981, p. 6. Adapted by permission of the Wisconsin Department of Public Instruction, 125 South Webster St., Madison, WI 53703.

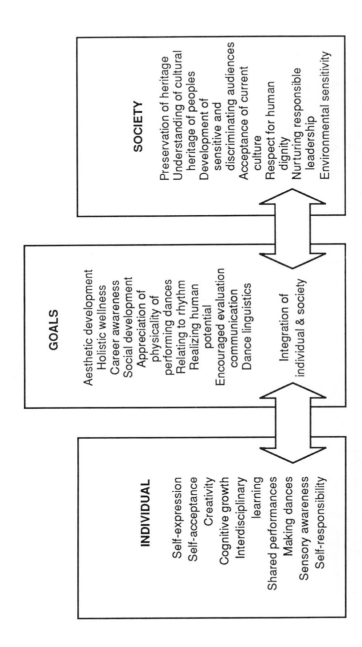

Figure 6.2. Wisconsin dance curriculum goals: Integration of individual and society. *Note.* From *Dance: Creative/Rhythmic Movement Education,* Bulletin No. 2119, 1981, p. 8. Adapted by permission of the Wisconsin Department of Public Instruction, 125 South Webster St., Madison, WI 53703.

The Wisconsin curriculum represents a hierarchic structure that describes the learning process for any age and provides a framework for organizing the learning experience. Local schools use the generalizations and variant concepts to develop their own curriculum. Additional concepts are identified as the teacher selects and organizes learning experiences that are appropriate and stimulating for students.

Ohio

Jan Hyatt, author of this curriculum guide, presents a creative movement curriculum which she designed to help the educator help the student find what she calls a balance (1985). This balance is central to the holistic approach that is employed in formulating the Ohio dance/movement curriculum. "Holistic problem-solving skills," Hyatt maintains, "can enhance the more traditional kinds of verbal and visual learning by developing a rationality along with global, non-linear, and intuitive strategies . . . . inherent in this balance is the fullest possible integration of thinking, feeling, and movement as they come together, stimulated by problem solving" (p. 43). This curriculum is tailored to elementary school children and consists of learning episodes that are designed around children's inherent urge to move. By thinking, feeling, and moving creatively, children enhance their self-concepts.

The curricular framework is theoretical and covers the notions of the body as an instrument for movement; the use of space, time, and energy; and the creation of relationships. The curriculum emphasizes the development of eight learning skills:

1. Concentration and focusing
2. Visual perception
3. Auditory perception
4. Spatial perception
5. Sequencing and memory
6. Time differentiation
7. Patterning
8. Creative problem solving

In addition to enhancing self-concept and developing the eight learning skills, the curriculum provides opportunities for students to explore, discover, and grow in the areas of psychomotor proficiency, aesthetics, and social responsibility. The guide includes sections about activities, movement elements, learning skills, special children, and environmental considerations.

The Ohio curriculum guide summarizes and defends its philosophy by stating, "This movement program must be child centered rather than lesson centered; creative movement centered rather than learning skill centered; and process rather than product oriented" (p. 262). It is a comprehensive document that serves as an effective springboard for both elementary school teachers and dance educators.

Alaska

The Alaska elementary school fine arts curriculum guide (Alaska Department of Education, 1985; see Table 6.1) is a flexible document that is subject to regular revision. The format is straightforward, but not oversimplified, and consists of topics/concepts, learning outcomes, and sample learning objectives. School districts that use this guide generate their own learning objectives within the framework of their district's topics/concepts and learning outcomes. The Alaska Department of Education states that this document is intended to "serve as a model, not a mandate" (p. iii). Individual variation is promoted while stressing the "collective responsibility for educating all students in Alaska" (p. iii).

Table 6.1   Framework of the Guide for the Dance Curriculum: Alaska

For the primary grades (grades 1-3), the following framework was developed:

Topic/Concept	Outcome Categories
Preliminary understandings	Listening, paying attention Following directions Dance safety
Qualities of movement in dance	Body awareness Spatial awareness Qualitative variations
Elements of rhythm in dance	Underlying beat, accent Moving in time to the music Rhythmic patterns, note values Expressing moods and feelings
Dance as a part of culture and heritage	Singing games and folk dances Awareness of different folk dances Specific Alaskan and other ethnic/tribal dances

For grades 4-8, the following framework was developed:

Qualities of movement in dance	Body awareness, spatial awareness, qualitative variations, introduction and development of relationships to others in dance
Elements of rhythm in dance	Meter and measure Phrasing Intensity, tempo Accompaniment
Creative expression in dance	Floor patterns Sequencing of moves and patterns Representation and interpretation

Topic/Concept	Outcome Categories
Dance as a part of culture and heritage	Values and history of ethnic and folk dances; appreciation of specific Alaskan and other ethnic/tribal dances
Enjoyment/skill/fitness	Cardiovascular and muscular fitness, feeling good about moving to music
Integration of dance with other arts	Dance as a vehicle or stimulus for other arts

Note. From *Elementary Fine Arts: Alaska Curriculum Guide* (p. 111) by the Alaska Department of Education, 1985, Juneau, AK: Alaska Department of Education. Copyright 1985 by the Alaska Department of Education. Reprinted by permission of the Alaska Department of Education, Office of Basic Education, P.O. Box F, Juneau, AK, 99811.

Dance education in Alaska seeks to integrate dance as a discrete art form into the entire curriculum. "Dance," according to the guide, "allows students of all levels and abilities to experiment and invent with movement, develop resources, make aesthetic judgements about dance, and begin to view dance from an [sic] historical perspective" (p. 43). Dance curriculum strives to help students realize their artistic potential through movement, and to this end, the Alaska curriculum guide identifies the following objectives:

1. To teach young people to dance
2. To help young people increase their awareness of their bodies and selves
3. To help young people enjoy dance and dancing
4. To help young people develop aesthetic awareness as they create
5. To help young people improve their sense of directionality, spatial orientation, and visual and kinesthetic perception

This framework shown in Table 6.1 is broken down into learning units comprised of a topic or concept with desirable learning outcomes plus one or more sample learning objectives (see Table 6.2). Teachers develop lesson plans from the learning units, taking into consideration their own special circumstances (e.g., class size, ability, moving space). The dance curriculum remains dynamic as the state regularly reviews and upgrades the curriculum guidelines and students and teachers adapt the learning units to suit their particular needs and aptitudes.

Table 6.2   Dance Curriculum Learning Unit, Grades 1-3: Alaska

Topic/Concept	Learning outcome *The learner will*	Sample learning objective *The learner will*
Dance as a part of culture and heritage	Know some Alaskan dances	Perform simple Alaskan regional dances
	Know some ethnic folk dances and singing games	Participate in dances and singing games of other cultures such as Mexican hat dance, square dance, tribal dances, etc.

Note. From *Elementary Fine Arts: Alaska Curriculum Guide* (p. 112) by the Alaska Department of Education, 1985, Juneau, AK: Alaska Department of Education. Copyright 1985 by the Alaska Department of Education. Reprinted by permission of the Alaska Department of Education, Office of Basic Education, P.O. Box F, Juneau, AK, 99811.

The Alaskan curriculum guide also stresses that experiences in dance can relate to and supplement other academic areas (e.g., mathematical concepts of shape, line, sequence, and ordinal numbers). To summarize, the Alaskan curriculum guide has been designed to develop the role of dance education and to provide justification for, and to sustain a sense of, dynamic growth and adaption in dance education.

Maryland

The curriculum guide for dance prepared by the Montgomery County Public Schools in Maryland is based on the belief that a curriculum embodies what teachers should teach and what students should learn (Montgomery County Public Schools, 1979). It contains prescribed elements that a dance program must follow, including course titles, codes, instructional objectives, content descriptions, prerequisites, time allotments, credit values, and an instructional point of view. However, the guidelines recognize a vital interaction necessary between the curriculum prescription and the efforts and applications of the individual schools. The specifications for dance are as follows:

1. Point of view—the reasons for studying dance
2. General information—explanations of how dance fulfills the county's educational goals

3. Description of program—a description and identification of the prescribed elements
4. Instructional guides—resources, bibliographies, teaching aids, etc.

Obligations imposed by the Maryland State Department of Education are the major influence on the Montgomery County curriculum and account in great part for its prescriptive approach. The two main obligations are accountability and graduation requirements.

The dance curriculum for Montgomery County Public Schools is not organized as a separate subject in Grades K-8 but is part of the elementary physical education program. At the high school level it is included in the requirement that schools provide aesthetic and arts education. Despite providing only limited curricular opportunities, the guide proposes that dance at all levels develops students' personal awareness, physical coordination, social skills, creative potential, and possible interests and talents in dance. During summer, the Montgomery County Public Schools offer advanced dance courses for gifted and talented students as part of an interrelated arts program.

Idaho

"Every child should be given quality dance experiences from Kindergarten to 12th Grade" (Idaho State Department of Education, 1978, p. 5). This quote illustrates the underlying philosophy of the state's dance curriculum guide, a philosophy that advocates a broad curriculum covering several styles and developed by qualified dance educators—a sound program with quality dance experiences taught by qualified teachers with strong dance backgrounds. The department of education maintains that dance is not only a discipline in itself but a proven tool for learning in the other academic areas, a tool that reinforces all learning and should be integrated into other curricula.

The structure of the curriculum is presented in the Tables 6.3 and 6.4. The curriculum guide lists goals and objectives with supporting comments and activities, and are meant to suggest, clarify, and be freely adapted as quality programming warrants.

Table 6.3   Dance Curriculum Goals: Idaho

Every child in Idaho should have the opportunity to

have a successful dance experience that generates further interest
have a varied dance experience
express ideas and emotions through dance movement

(Cont.)

Table 6.3   (Continued)

Every child in Idaho should have the opportunity to

develop a musical sense through movement

develop discriminating awareness of movement as an artistic medium

develop an appreciation of dance as an art form

experience dance as an additional choice in the arts

develop an appreciation of our dance heritage, both ritual and historic

understand the discipline involved in training a dancer

be exposed to the career opportunities associated with dance

develop desirable social relationships

discover the relationship between self and body

develop an adequate degree of satisfaction in moving with control

experience the pleasure, confidence, and self-esteem resulting from moving with control

realize his or her creative potential

promote his or her perceptual-motor development through dance movement

recognize that the elements of dance are the elements of life

Note. From *Dance: A Guide for Idaho Public Schools. Grades K–12* (p. 20) by the Idaho State Department of Education, 1978, Boise, ID: Idaho State Department of Education, Division of Instructional Improvement. Copyright 1978 by the Idaho State Department of Education. Reprinted by permission.

Table 6.4   Dance Curriculum Objectives: Idaho

Each child should

develop and refine a movement memory

be able to relate movement effectively to accompanying sounds and music

demonstrate increased strength, flexibility, and coordination

experience and be able to recognize styles of dance

be able to demonstrate an understanding of several historical and cultural perspectives of dance

develop a broader range of movement and increased movement vocabulary

see live and filmed dance performances

participate with others

give form to creative impulses

Each child should

perform in front of peers

learn to look at dance critically

draw motivation for movement experiences from various stimuli

synthesize life experiences into dance

integrate dance into the other arts, sciences, and humanities

Note. From *Dance: A Guide for Idaho Public Schools. Grades K–12* (p. 23) by the Idaho State Department of Education, 1978, Boise, ID: Idaho State Department of Education, Division of Instructional Improvement. Copyright 1978 by the Idaho State Department of Education. Reprinted by permission.

The Idaho State Department of Education advocates integrating dance with subjects such as health, science, math, language arts, music, social studies, English, business, and psychology and provides specific suggestions to accomplish this objective.

The curriculum guide suggests that an elementary curriculum include creative dance, dance songs and stories, folk dance, square dance, and social dance, all of which should be offered in a way that ensures the student will always have new dance experiences to look forward to. The guide suggests that dance in secondary schools be offered as an elective, as part of a fine arts course, or in conjunction with a musical production. High school curriculum may include modern, ballet, jazz, theater dance, tap, folk, square, and social dance. Quality is emphasized for both elementary and high school curricula.

New Zealand

New Zealand's educational philosophy and most of its practices are based on the British system of schooling, which is known for its formality, depth, and narrow scope of subjects. New Zealand's dance curriculum is likewise structured and analytical, with all components meticulously interlocked and the overall appearance architecturally formal. But despite the rigid outward appearance, much flexibility and creativity occur in the dance classes. Dance activities have always been guaranteed a place in New Zealand's elementary education, thus the curriculum guidelines do not provide a rationale for dance in education. "Movement," according to the New Zealand Department of Education (1977), "is characteristic of human beings. Children's understanding of movement can be improved if they are allowed to explore it" (p. 2).

The curriculum guide for movement and dance activities lists the following six objectives:

1. To develop skill in movement
2. To assist intellectual development
3. To stimulate the senses and develop aesthetic appreciation
4. To develop a means of expression and communication
5. To develop creative ability
6. To introduce a form of recreation that children may continue in their own time

Based on these objectives, an overall instructional plan is designed that can consist of one large block, several smaller blocks, or weekly/daily sessions throughout the year (see Figure 6.3). These plans are structured to be developmental and include an objective, an approach (e.g., rhythmic, mimetic or dance), and developmental stages. A sense of integration pervades the instructional plan, emphasizing that dance makes a contribution to the physical, intellectual, aesthetic, emotional, and social development of the student. The guide provides sample lesson plans further illustrating the structural approach to curricular planning.

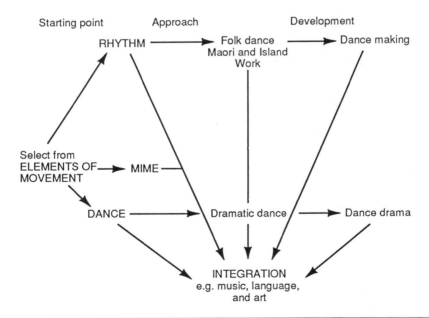

Figure 6.3. Suggestions for development: New Zealand. *Note.* Reprinted by permission of the Department of Education, Wellington, New Zealand. From *Physical Education-standard 2-form 2. Movement and Dance Activities*, 1977, p. 4.

Establishment and enrichment of a movement language is a critical component of the dance curriculum and the lesson plans. According to the New Zealand Department of Education, "Before children can express themselves satisfactorily through movement, a 'vocabulary' is necessary. . . . They should become familiar by name and experience with the elements which affect movement and realize that the possibilities are endless" (p. 9). Of equal importance is the ability to analyze movement, a skill that is thought to help children become aware of movement and learn to move skillfully in a variety of ways.

The role of dance in the context of the entire curriculum is illustrated in Figure 6.4.

The New Zealand curriculum guide stresses that for students to dance they must possess a dance vocabulary, have control of their bodies, feel confident in using their bodies, and be involved in what they are doing. Only then are they able to explore a mood, idea, or feeling; select appropriate movements from their vocabularies; and join these to form sequences that are expressions for them and perhaps have meaning for others. These aptitudes are developed through movement analysis and a structured curriculum.

Conclusions

The dance art struggles for recognition (and sometimes existence) in today's schools. Despite Elliot Eisner's cogent argument supporting the vital role of the arts in education most state departments of education have given only cursory attention to the value of arts education. Dance is often overshadowed by other subjects and is rarely granted comparable status or curricular equality. However, once a dance component has been established and legislated, the curricula that result are typically well planned and presented. These dance curricula are based on sound dance education philosophy and include every activity and skill possible. The sampling of state dance curriculum guides included in this chapter clearly demonstrates that the dance discipline is broad, salient, and varied, yet is not so unwieldy that it cannot be readily organized into teachable concepts and topics with corresponding learning objectives and evaluative methods. This is a credit to the dance education profession.

The delivery system for dance education, including its curricular content and message, has an impact on the effectiveness of dance teaching and learning. No two dance teachers will teach alike even when using identical curricular material. Each dance teacher judges the best way to arrange, deliver, and evaluate the material and in this manner prepares and monitors the dance learner's experiences. Quality education depends on competent teachers, thus a method of ensuring teacher quality is needed.

How is the quality of dance teaching maintained? Who monitors and evaluates the dance teacher and with what tools or methods? What are the resources available to dance teachers whose teaching methodologies need upgrading, strengthening, assessment, or feedback? Chapter 7 addresses these issues.

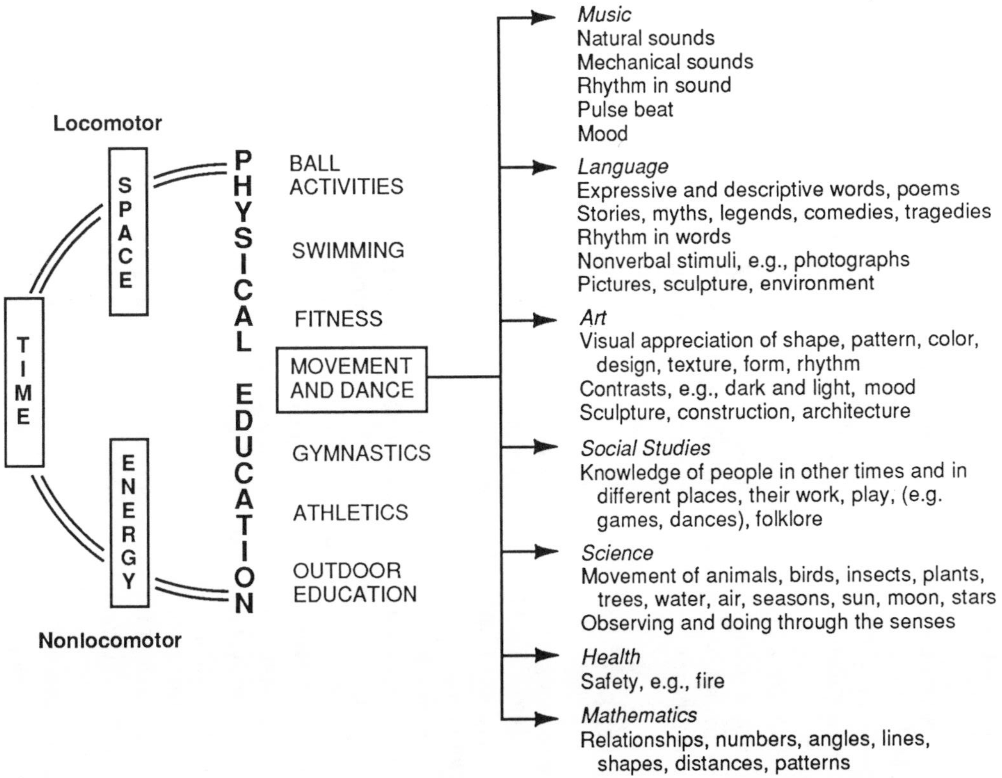
Locomotor
SPACE
TIME
ENERGY
Nonlocomotor
PHYSICAL EDUCATION
BALL ACTIVITIES
SWIMMING
FITNESS
MOVEMENT AND DANCE
GYMNASTICS
ATHLETICS
OUTDOOR EDUCATION
Music
Natural sounds
Mechanical sounds
Rhythm in sound
Pulse beat
Mood
Language
Expressive and descriptive words, poems
Stories, myths, legends, comedies, tragedies
Rhythm in words
Nonverbal stimuli, e.g., photographs
Pictures, sculpture, environment
Art
Visual appreciation of shape, pattern, color, design, texture, form, rhythm
Contrasts, e.g., dark and light, mood
Sculpture, construction, architecture
Social Studies
Knowledge of people in other times and in different places, their work, play, (e.g. games, dances), folklore
Science
Movement of animals, birds, insects, plants, trees, water, air, seasons, sun, moon, stars
Observing and doing through the senses
Health
Safety, e.g., fire
Mathematics
Relationships, numbers, angles, lines, shapes, distances, patterns

Figure 6.4. Summary of integration throughout curriculum. *Note.* Reprinted by permission of the Department of Education, Wellington, New Zealand. From *Physical Education-standard 2-form 2. Movement and Dance Activities*, 1977, p. 67.

Key Terms

Cognition—the mental process by which knowledge is gained

Curriculum—a course of study offered by a particular field and also the total courses offered by an educational institution

Curriculum guidelines—policies or procedures governing course offerings

Discrete art—an art that is distinct and separate from the other arts

Dynamic—emphasizing continuous change and activity

Fitness—the state of being physically sound

Holistic—emphasizing the importance of the whole and the interdependence of its parts

Movement vocabulary—a repertoire or reserve of movement techniques

Prescriptive—emphasizing rules, directions, and customs

Quality—distinguished by excellence or superiority

Skill development—the development of techniques requiring specialized ability and training

Social culturization—the process of transmitting social values by means of artistic and intellectual activities

Starting points—points of origin

Structural analytical—elemental parts separated and arranged in an organized format

Student Activities and Assignments

1. Obtain your state's curriculum guidelines for dance education. Identify the mission statement, the learning objectives, the topics, concepts, or content areas, and the evaluation procedures.
2. Explain what is meant by "dance as a discrete art" when it is referred to in the context of a school's overall education curriculum.
3. Discuss your own views on Elliot Eisner's contention that "the arts are not mere diversions from the important business of education; they are essential resources." Substantiate and illustrate your argument with examples from the dance discipline.

Further Reading

Eisner, E. (1982). *Cognition and curriculum: A basic for deciding what to teach.* New York: Longman.

Ritson, R.J. (1986). Creative dance: A systematic approach to teaching children. *Journal of Physical Education, Recreation and Dance,* **57**(3), 67-78.

Russell, J. (1975). *Creative dance in the primary school* (2nd ed.). Plymouth, England: MacDonald & Evans.

Chapter 7
Supervision of Dance Teachers

"Unfortunately the best instruction is provided for the people who probably need it the least—professional dancers. Children are exposed to dancing teachers of all degrees of quality and may be taught poor techniques and develop lifetime problems" (Bergfield, 1982, p. 103).

To my knowledge no guidelines, texts, or publications address the supervision of dance teachers in the schools, despite the fact that thousands of public and private schools across the country employ dance education professionals and hold them accountable. Moreover, I have never encountered such practices as clinical supervision, timeline coding, and mirroring the classroom in the context of dance instruction. As most administrators are not knowledgeable about dance instruction, they typically do not closely supervise experienced dance teachers. Experienced dance teachers, in turn, often do not closely supervise student teachers and may even readily turn over a class of would-be dancers to a novice teacher.

In some schools dance instruction is supervised and reviewed collectively with physical education and coaching. This chapter argues that while some teacher behaviors, planning strategies, and learning outcomes are common to all school content areas, dance demands additional, unique consideration and is best served by a modified version of a clinical supervision model. This model offers the dance education field a flexible framework for improving instruction, promoting professional development, and sustaining job satisfaction.

Terms and Assumptions

In this section, the term *dance* (as a content area in the schools) encompasses dance technique, composition, performance, and the creative art process (Shuker, 1985). This definition assumes that dance is taught by certified dance teachers who have been educated in college dance major programs or who hold a dance minor and a related teaching major (e.g., physical education). Dance teachers in this context are classified in the following groups:

- Dance majors
- Physical education majors with a dance minor
- Art, music, or drama majors with a dance minor
- Elementary education classroom teachers in dance
- Dance education specialists
- Guest artists (artists in the schools)

This discussion assumes that these dance teachers operate under a prescribed dance curriculum that has been approved by the school district and includes unit or block plans and a system of lesson planning and evaluation. (Unfortunately, many school dance programs deteriorate into a single unit or block taught once a year, usually folk dancing. Exemplary curriculum models are available, but well-researched curriculum planning techniques and theories are not often implemented.)

Gray (1984b) defines *dance teaching* as "the dynamic, interactive process of transmitting the skills and knowledge of dance. Further, it is the total or aggregate influence, appropriate or inappropriate, that a dance teacher imposes on students in an instructional (rather than a choreographic or rehearsal) activity situation" (p. 154).

This definition assumes a background of teacher training, some dance performance experience, and considerable role modeling. It also assumes that in the absence of role modeling and in-service training, the dance teacher is properly supervised in the schools and is subsequently eligible for promotion, merit, and tenure. As mentioned earlier, this is seldom true. Supervision of dance teachers generally consists of the rare occasions when the principal or department head enters the studio or gym or vacated cafeteria, observes the class for a short while, slips out unnoticed, and later submits a cursory evaluation. A distance is maintained between dance teacher and supervisor, and no attempt is made to relate the evaluation to job or program improvement. Clinical supervision, however, involves a close and ongoing collaboration between teacher and supervisor. The remainder of this chapter presents the cyclic process of supervision with adaptions pertaining to the special needs and considerations of dance instruction in the school setting.

The Clinical Supervision Process

This kind of supervision is primarily concerned with helping the teacher improve teaching performance (see Figure 7.1). Weller (1971) said *clinical supervision* is "focused upon the improvement of instruction by means of systematic cycles of planning, observation, and intensive intellectual analysis of actual teaching performance in the interest of rational modification" (p. 20). The phases, factors, and goals of this process are presented in the following sections.

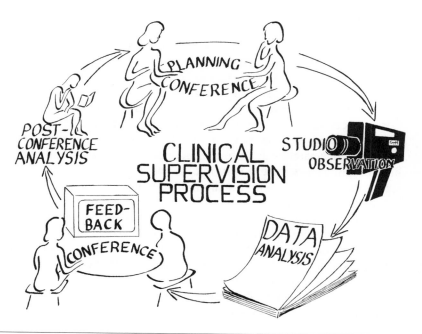

Figure 7.1. Clinical supervision process.

Phases

The clinical supervision process is divided into five phases, each of which is critical to the overall success of the system, success being defined as increased professional development. These phases are as follows:

1. *Planning conference*—ensures a nonhostile, collaborative environment in which dance teacher and supervisor can communicate. At this conference the teacher shares his or her unique teaching situation and style of teaching, and decisions are made concerning specific teacher and learner behaviors to be observed and the type of data-gathering method to be used. The teacher's lesson plans can be reviewed during the conference, and past, present, and future dance classes should be discussed so the observer understands the chronological and developmental context of the class. Clarification is the key objective of the phase.
2. *Studio observation*—uses wide range of observational techniques to capture dance teaching data. As dance instruction typically takes place in a large, open space, use of a wide lens camera is the most effective method for recording class activity. In order to unobtrusively capture a broad picture (and later extract the critical behaviors) a video camera can be mounted and a small wireless microphone can be attached to the leotard of the teacher, thus recording both verbal and nonverbal behaviors. Another method involves tracking the location behaviors of the teacher by combining video feedback and an electronic spacing detector (Gray, 1984a). The teacher is later provided with a map of his or her movement patterns. Observing what teachers and students say to each other is as important as how, when, and where they move during the dance class. The data collected is only as valid as the instrument used to collect it, and it thus behooves the supervisor and the dance teacher to carefully select the most appropriate instrument.
3. *Data analysis*—provides opportunities for the supervisor and the dance teacher to separately analyze the data collected during the studio observation. Viewing the videotape and listening to the audiotape (with or without a transcription) will familiarize both the teacher and the supervisor with the amount and significance of the recorded information. Computer data analysis software is available for use with video and audio recordings. Both teacher and supervisor should take objective notes of the predetermined behaviors; these notes could include incidence, duration, pace, sequence, and proximities.
4. *Feedback conference*—provides opportunity for teacher and supervisor to cooperatively analyze the data and reach an agreement about its implications. The dance teacher and the supervisor interpret the data by discussing their reactions, with particular emphasis on the dance teacher's opinions and feelings. The dance teacher and the supervisor

decide on future changes, modifications, and actions. These changes may include ideas for varying the teaching style, music selections, closure activities, and safety factors.

5. *Post-conference analysis*—sets the stage for the clinical supervision cycle to begin again. This conference focuses on job improvement goals, rather than on immediate teaching modifications or changes to lesson plans and student outcomes. The dance teacher is encouraged through self-analysis and contemplation to formulate future plans for his or her career as a dance educator. He or she may focus on a certain dance technique or on the creative process. Agreement on a constructive self-improvement plan results in the need for a later planning conference, and thus the cycle begins again.

Factors

The essential characteristics and assumptions of a clinical supervision model for dance teachers revolve around the desire for teaching performance improvement (see Figure 7.2). Factors for successful supervision include the following:

- Supervisory focus on constructive analysis and reinforcement
- Self-perpetuating cycle of planning, teaching, and analysis
- Clear, objective, and unbiased observational evidence
- Assumption that supervision is a dynamic process in which dance teacher and supervisor collaborate
- Freedom for dance teachers to analyze and improve their own teaching and develop their own styles
- Freedom for supervisors to do likewise with their respective supervisory styles
- Belief that improvement of dance instruction requires teachers to learn specific intellectual, physical, and behavioral/affective skills
- Belief that dance teaching effectiveness is attainable

Goals

Planning conferences, observations, data analysis, feedback conferences, post-conference analyses, and goal setting are the major activities of clinical supervision. By these means, the professional development of dance teachers is promoted. The aims of clinical supervision are as follows (Acheson & Gall, 1980):

1. To provide dance teachers with objective feedback on the current state of their instruction. What dance teachers perceive they are doing in the dance studio may be quite different from what the data supports.

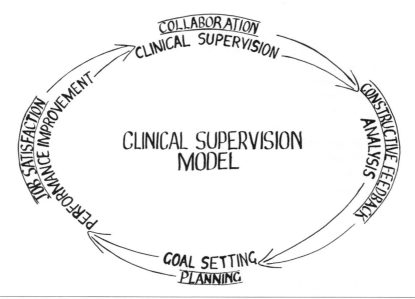

Figure 7.2.   Goals of clinical supervision.

For example, dance teachers may believe that they are clearly visible to all the students as they demonstrate. Observations suggest, however, that students in the back rows imitate students in front of them, thus receiving the movement information secondhand.

2. To diagnose and solve instructional problems. Conference techniques and observational data help dance teachers pinpoint specific discrepancies between what they do and what they should do. For example, a dance teacher who is unable to identify each student by name should be advised to use name tags or devise other means to aid name recall.

3. To help teachers develop skill in using instructional strategies. Instructional strategies are teacher behaviors that form patterns and episodes and which are effective in promoting learning (e.g., motivating students, managing the studio environment, or selecting teaching aids and materials). For example, research has shown that effective teachers allow their students more engaged time (time spent in moving and dancing) than less effective teachers (Metzler, 1981). A time engaged in dancing (TED) data gathering and analysis experiment can be easily conducted to determine the amount of time students are immersed in actual learning activities in the dance studio.

4. To evaluate teachers for promotion, tenure, or other decisions. At some stage dance teachers, along with other school faculty, must be evaluated for retention or promotion. The advantage of the clinical supervi-

sion cycle is that throughout the program the dance teacher is intimately involved in the supervision process and is given opportunities to improve her or his performance. Moreover, feelings of hostility or resentment are tempered because of the sharing and collaborative behaviors that are integrated into the cycle.

5. To help teachers develop a positive attitude about professional development. Dance training is never completed; dance teacher certification does not signify the end of learning about dance, keeping the body in good condition, or experiencing aesthetic and cultural awakenings. Dance teachers in the schools need to view themselves as professionals in the dance field, just as dance company members do. They must be encouraged to engage in self-development activities and continued skill training as a career-long effort.

Clinical supervision should ultimately improve learning. By improving teaching performance, student performance will also improve, creating another cycle. Thus dance educators in dance teacher training programs should become familiar with the clinical supervision model and integrating the process into dance pedagogy curricula. Meanwhile, a number of informal and less clinical strategies can be used by dance teachers and their supervisors to build closer working relationships that will in turn affect students. Because of their informality, these relationships are better defined as *partnerships*.

Nonclinical Supervision Partnerships

Much teacher supervision is not as structured as the clinical supervision process. Supervision results from a productive partnership between teachers and those in supervisory roles (e.g., department head, chairperson, senior faculty, school principal, or student teaching supervisor). A productive supervisory relationship gives students as well as others in the institution a sense of the worth and credibility of the dance program. Professional partnerships between teachers and supervisors are based on sound human relations strategies, which are not necessarily clinical. The partnerships grow in strength and consistency, to the immense benefit of dance students. Some of the more notable proven strategies are as follows.

Clear Expectations

The supervisor should clarify her expectations about organization, appearance, preparatory materials, procedures, and responsibilities. The supervisor's directions should be lucid and complete, specifying subject matter and location and duration of class.

Open Communication

The supervisor and the teacher should keep the channels of communication open, sharing information and concerns to improve everyone's effectiveness. The teacher needs up-to-the-minute information from the supervisor on matters ranging from teaching aids to aesthetics. Student teachers should meet with the supervisor and the cooperating teacher, and student teachers as a whole should meet regularly to share class experiences with each other. Supervisors from different disciplines should meet regularly as well. Sheryl Goodes at the University of Wisconsin-Madison coordinates highly successful monthly campus-wide meetings of the student teaching supervisors from all disciplines, thus maintaining open communication across the specialities.

Mutual Understanding of Goals and Objectives

Teachers who understand the goals and objectives of their school's dance program are more likely to cooperate in attaining them. Supervisors should explain the general mission and function of the dance program or department so teachers will better understand their roles and responsibilities, and more positive and productive teamwork will result.

Input

Input should come from both cooperating and student teachers. Cooperating teachers should make suggestions about procedures and policies, while student teachers should suggest improvements or changes in teaching practicum arrangements. Both supervisors and teachers should be recognized for designing new and better guidelines, particularly if the program has no uniform method or materials. When students, teachers, and supervisors are given the chance to discuss school or departmental problems and proposed changes, the dance program as a whole benefits—supervised teaching experiences are less threatening and teachers are more willing to accept critiques and decisions. Commitment to work toward personal and program goals increases as value is placed on individual input.

Delegation of Responsibility

A supervisor who feels confident about delegating certain tasks to a teacher is freer to concentrate on other aspects of his or her dance education responsibilities. The teacher responds by feeling more competent and in control. Successful relationships between supervisor and dance teacher are based on trust in one another to assume increasing responsibility and accountability.

Positive Attitude and Praise

Dance teachers are more effective and more motivated if they know that their teaching and class management skills are satisfactory or better. They are encouraged if their students let them know that they are appreciated and valuable and that their instructional mode is working. A positive attitude on the part of the supervisor also is essential. Teachers and supervisors should reward outstanding work with praise and, if appropriate, a written commendation. Teachers should keep a special file of teaching accomplishments and successes to be used for motivation and career advancement.

Constructive Criticism

Criticism of unsatisfactory performance in the classroom, gym, or studio should be designed to improve future performance. The supervisor should explain in detail why she is not pleased with the lesson, remembering to criticize the result of the problem and not the teacher. The teacher should then be given the chance to respond to the supervisor's observations. Both parties should contribute suggestions and recommendations on improving the situation in the future. Criticism of a dance teaching problem should not be regarded as a setback, but rather as a step forward.

Conclusions

Supervision of dance education professionals is not an end in itself, but rather an unending and self-generating process that enriches and strengthens the dance teaching field and ensures the quality of the teaching/learning process. Most importantly, it is a process beneficial to teachers, administrators, and students, between whom relationships have changed dramatically in recent years. Supervisors and teachers are now likely to be colleagues and collaborators, while students now rely on their teachers for far more than academic and artistic direction. Chapter 8 addresses these new trends and introduces the reader to a new concept in dance education—pastoral care for dance students and their teachers.

Key Terms

Certified dance teachers—teachers of dance who have met the state's requirements to practice their profession

Clinical supervision—the objective observation and diagnosis of performance

Constructive criticism—discriminating judgements and evaluations that are positive and helpful in nature

Cooperating teacher—the teacher whose classes are the laboratory for student teachers

Feedback—the return of information about the result of a process

Input—the contribution to, or participation in, a common effort

Nonclinical supervision—the subjective observation and analysis of performance

Open communication—the free and unrestricted exchange of thoughts, messages, or information

Partnerships—association of people in an activity of common interest

Prescribed dance curriculum—a course of dance study approved by an educational or state institution

Student teacher—noncertified teacher trainee

Studio observation—act of watching activity in a dance studio or moving space

Supervision—the direction and inspection of performance

Student Activities and Assignments

1. Clearly define the roles and responsibilities of the participants in the clinical supervision of dance teachers. Include the supervisor, cooperating teacher, teacher, school principal or department head (if different from the supervisor), and students.
2. List some professional self-development activities in which dance teachers should be continually involved, and explain their importance.
3. Research and list at least five techniques for observing classroom teacher behaviors. Signify which, if any, of these are appropriate for observing dance teacher behaviors.
4. List the common factors and requirements for building and maintaining mutually productive relationships between teachers and students, teachers and supervisors, and teachers and teachers. Reference your response to the dance profession.

Further Reading

Acheson, K. A., & Gall, M. D. (1980). *Techniques in the clinical supervision of teachers*. New York: Longman.
Blumberg, A. (1974). *Supervisors and teachers: A private cold war*. Berkeley, CA: McCutchan.

Chapter 8
Support Services and Pastoral Care

Gone are the days when dance teachers related to students only during the time spent in class and when student advising simply meant approving schedules and outlining graduation requirements. Today's teachers realize that there is much more to teaching than just showing up for class; indeed, teachers who involve themselves with student growth and development practice their profession under optimal conditions and garner optimal rewards.

Many of the barriers that traditionally separated students from teachers, teachers from administrators, and teachers from professional dancers and choreographers have disappeared. Educators now concern themselves with much more than the mere academic care of students; this is particularly true in dance education, as dance impinges on virtually all aspects of a person's well-being—social, physical, cultural, intellectual, psychological, and aesthetic. This chapter presents and describes a *pastoral care* agenda for dance programs, a relatively new concept that provides the articulation needed to integrate dance students into the educational, technological, and artistic components of society.

Pastoral care of dance students is attention to and concern for their nonacademic needs, such as emotional, social, vocational, and health needs. Pastoral care providers are not to be confused with professionals in psychotherapy, medicine, crisis intervention, career placement, or financial aid, although these professionals are frequently utilized for referrals and are indispensable to a well-operated pastoral care program. A pastoral care program for dance must be specifically designed for and by each institution, utilizing counseling, support services, special programs, referrals, and information networks.

An almost endless number of topics and concerns qualify for inclusion on the pastoral care agenda. Ideal pastoral care programs are flexible, dynamic, and adaptable. The items that follow are care areas that particularly apply to dance students and generally apply to individual dance programs. Dance teachers and administrators are advised to add, subtract, and modify to suit their programs' needs.

Injury Prevention and Health Maintenance

Research on the functioning and malfunctioning of the human body has recently crept into dance literature. The early research was spurred by access to the biomechanic and exercise physiology laboratories of physical education departments. Research since the 1970s has accelerated due to computers, electronic recording devices, and a national obsession with fitness and health. Information on dance injury prevention has spawned events from in-house workshops to national and international symposia. Much of this information, according to Sandra Minton (1987), has been expressly leveled at dance teachers "to help them understand the proper conditioning and effective use of the body. . . . The science of human movement has been joined with the art for the purpose of producing dancers who are stronger, better conditioned, and more safe and effective" (p. 30).

Teachers charged with the pastoral care of dance students should be aware that most dance injuries occur during and after adolescence. Most dance injuries are not sudden and rarely require immediate surgery but rather are chronic and result from a history of increasingly inefficient movement patterns. Muscles are typically misused rather than unused or overused, which increases likelihood of a dance injury. Certified movement analyst Sandra Kau Lauffenburger (1987) adds: "Finally muscle imbalance results and added to excessive stress (repetitive use) and fatigue, the ingredients for dance injury exist" (p. 58).

No pastoral care program should be without adequate information and support services concerning prevention and treatment of dance injuries. Closely associated with this concern is general health care. The University of California at Irvine uses a unique health screening process whereby the majority of dance students who participate in dance classes beyond the beginning year undergo a thorough examination by a team of experts. The students are weighed, measured, and calipered for body fat and are asked to fill out a health fact sheet (see Figure 8.1). When the student is ill or injured he or she is medically advised and then carefully monitored to ensure a full recovery before resuming training. A process such as this combined with a close collaboration with the school health center meets the health maintenance provisions of pastoral care. All dance programs would benefit from a comparable unit in their own operation.

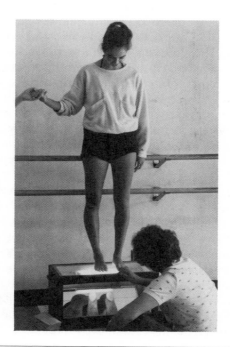

Figure 8.1.   Dance student being screened. *Note.* Photo courtesy of Janice Gudde Plastino.

Career Guidance

Most dance educators are expected to provide career guidance information to students. This responsibility is not limited to higher education, where young adults prepare to enter the work world, but is also found in high schools, where talented dancers demand support and direction in order to embark on performance careers and to train for other dance-related professions. Some students who need career guidance are re-entering the dance field after an absence, while others are undergoing midcareer changes and are opting for dance or dance-related job training opportunities through extended (continuing) education and community education programs. The responsibility for supplying pastoral care in these cases often lies with qualified and experienced dance teachers and administrators, who have several options.

One option for meeting these needs is through restructuring or augmenting the dance curriculum, which can be achieved in two ways. The first way is to supplement each dance course offering with pertinent vocational information (e.g., ballet classes could incorporate readings, guest speakers, community assignments, and investigations on ballet career opportunities). The other way is to offer seminars or workshops that address dance careers, job hunting, resume preparation, portfolio design, and interviewing. During my involvement with the University of Wisconsin-Madison dance program, I offered such a workshop and had to repeat it several times because it was so popular among dance education students. At the University of Arizona in Tucson, Dr. John Wilson conducted a minicourse in dance career preparation that included producing portfolio videotapes and actually applying for dance positions.

Another option for providing pastoral care is to ensure that the school's vocational guidance service is adequately supplied with information on dance and dance-related careers. This information should include announcements and descriptions of vacancies, auditions, internships, fellowships, grants, and classified positions. A number of journals and newsletters regularly announce dance and arts opportunities. A few of these are *The Chronicle of Higher Education, The National Arts Job Bank, Education Jobs, UPDATE,* and *Education Week.* Each state publishes job listings (e.g., *California Job Journal*) while most college placement services release weekly or monthly job bulletins (e.g., the University of Arizona's *Employment Opportunities in Education*). Current issues of these journals and bulletins should be available in campus careers offices. Much of this career information can also be provided on bulletin boards in studios and locker rooms; this is important when guidance services are limited or nonexistent.

A final option, which involves campus- or school-wide cooperation, is to provide more interdisciplinary programs that focus on the career goals of dancers. By expanding their curricular horizons, dance students will inevitably come in contact with opportunities that are obscured in a comparatively narrow dance major program, and they will thus broaden their career avenues. Restrictive specialization in dance must be discouraged. James O. Freedman (1987), president of Dartmouth College, said in his 1987 inaugural address:

Too often, the increasing tendency toward specialization has had fragmenting consequences for the life of the mind. It has sheltered men and women of broad-ranging imagination behind narrowly drawn disciplinary bounds, thereby discouraging them from becoming educated in the fullest sense of that worthy term. It has reduced the opportunities for collegial discourse among faculty and students from different departments and disciplines, as each has become the master of material of more slender scope. And it has denied faculty and students an understanding of the premises and assumptions of disciplines other than their own, thereby inhibiting inquiry across disciplinary lines. (p. 47)

Fortunately, college students in all disciplines are demanding more customized programs of study and more individualized degrees, a trend that many hope will invade the high schools as well. The arts are leading the way in demonstrating that curricula can be effectively redesigned and adapted to the needs and ambitions of dancers and other artists.

Viable dance careers can be sought through avenues other than college and high school courses and curricula. Cooperative education and work experience programs are prime examples of alternate routes. Dance students, like other creative and determined persons, can design their own job experiences. *What Color is Your Parachute?* by Richard Nelson Bolles outlines more career strategies; this book is listed at the end of this chapter as a recommendation for further reading.

Specific issues regarding dance careers are ably addressed in an article by Sandi Combest, Cynthia Wiese, and Irma Caton (1986), who base their discussion on a demographic survey they conducted from 1980 to 1982 to determine the trends in undergraduate degree programs. The key question that the researchers posed to dance teachers in higher education was, "What do you anticipate are the future prospects for nonteaching options or alternate career programs in the dance program at your university?" The discussion that resulted from the survey was revealing, and passages are reproduced here because of their relevance to pastoral care programming. Combest, Wiese, and Caton ask:

What are we preparing all these dance students to do—dance? As educators who have developed dance programs at colleges and universities, we should assume some responsibility for providing alternative dance-related career opportunities. Many of the students who major in dance have little concern about their futures when they enter the program. Proper guidance of students would enable them to better understand future opportunities and make them aware of alternate dance-related career possibilities. (p. 74)

The responses to the survey showed a lack of knowledge and imagination, and dance or movement therapy was listed as the major alternative career option. Table 8.1 provides a list of possible careers for dance teachers and students; Marr (1975) also lists alternate careers in dance.

Pastoral care provision for dance career guidance comprises, but is not limited to, advising students to create or investigate alternatives, providing information, and supporting both traditional and nontraditional options. According

Table 8.1 Dance Careers: A Listing of Possible Markets

Obvious	Less obvious
Teaching	Technology
Therapy	Liturgical dance
Notation	Shadow theatre
Lighting design	Library collections
Costuming	Dance sales and marketing
Arts administration	Photography
Acting	Architecture (studio design)
Film industry	Anthropology
Mime	Corporate fitness
Video dance	Health industry
Adaptive dance	Dance illustrator
Writing	Retirement community
Stage management	Figure skating
Research	Gymnastics
Dance criticism	Arts foundations
Exercise physiology	International exchanges
Television	Journalism

to Combest, Wiese, and Caton, "We as dance educators must join our students in projecting into the future by providing viable alternate dance-related career options" (p. 77). Dance is still regarded as a gender-specific field; in this country in particular, the acceptance of men and boys in dance is qualified at best. Pastoral care activities can improve this situation, which is discussed in the next section.

Sexual Politics

The dance field shows more sex disparity than any other art. Dance is still seen as a feminine art, whereas music, fine arts, theater, and opera are perceived as more neutral or asexual. In dance departments of schools with approximately equal numbers of male and female students (where often the dance program is housed in physical education and athletic departments) women outnumber men by extreme proportions. In 1984 , campus-wide auditions for the annual dance production at California Polytechnic State University attracted 70 women and only 5 men. Ironically, increasing numbers of women are entering traditionally male-dominated fields, but there is little evidence that the reverse is true.

What pastoral care activities are appropriate for this situation? *Inreach* activities (i.e., institution-based remedies) and *outreach* activities (e.g., aggressive recruiting, community action, male artists-in-schools programming, and increased visibility of male dancers) are the answers. NFL players Riki Ellison (see Figure 8.2) of the San Francisco 49ers and Lynn Swann of the Pittsburgh Steelers both studied dance at the University of Southern California while playing football for that school, and both men continue to attend dance concerts and take an occasional class. Both have expressed an interest in using their own sports visibility to promote dance for boys and men, a progressive step toward revising dance's gender-related image.

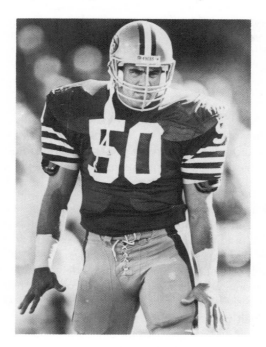

Figure 8.2. Riki Ellison of the San Francisco 49ers. *Note.* Photo courtesy of Riki Ellison.

Body therapist A.A. Leath of Madison, Wisconsin, says that few males enroll even in creative classes in which the individual is encouraged to develop his own style of movement. Most of the boys who do enroll soon drop out, except in rare cases in which boys receive unusual support from both parents who believe in the enjoyment of movement. Ellen Jacob (1981) maintains that the number of boys enrolled in ballet classes tripled between 1965 and 1980, but the total figure is still probably very small.

Dance teachers must give the same or often more support to the boys and men in dance classes. Teachers must provide an atmosphere of encouragement and acceptance; all dance activities should be made accessible; and opportunities should be provided for men and boys to express their own special rhythms and imagery. These then are examples of inreach activities. To ensure that dance for boys and men is universally accepted and recognized, extensive outreach activities must also be planned and implemented. Most of these activities will involve bolstering the image of male dancers, which will be achieved most readily through the media and through school organizations such as the Parent-Teacher Association. As more boys and men become dancers, more male teachers and choreographers will be available. These leaders will in turn encourage more boys and men to dance, and they will also create more dance styles, techniques, and teaching strategies that express the masculine point of view. Although male dance will always be somewhat different from female dance, the two can evolve into a more equitable coexistence.

Other Agenda Items

Following is a list of actual and perceived nonacademic needs of dance students. Literature and resources are available in most cases. I welcome further suggestions and information regarding these agenda items so that strong and practicable pastoral care programs for dance students can be built.

1. *Stress management*—Students and teachers of dance are subject to physical, mental, and emotional stress. While these often don't warrant a visit to a medical practitioner or psychotherapist, alternative methods should be available to manage stress. The following methods are useful and are generally available to dance personnel: meditation, autogenics, biofeedback, massage, Alexander technique, yoga, and peer or professional counseling. Pastoral care providers should be trained to detect early symptoms of stress in their students so that problems can be dealt with before the stress worsens.
2. *Substance abuse programs*—Unfortunately, dancers sometimes respond to pressures by using alcohol, tobacco, or drugs. Substance abuse is as common among professional dancers as it is among professional athletes. An effective pastoral care program for dance provides information about appropriate treatment programs in the community or on campus.
3. *Eating disorder treatment*—Dancers' obsession with shape and weight has led to a disproportionate incidence of severe eating disorders among this population. Research has revealed that ballet dancers especially

resort to fasting, self-induced vomiting, laxatives, diuretics, and dangerous diets in order to stay or get thin. Anorexia nervosa, a form of severe voluntary starvation that can lead to death, is more common among dancers than other students. A dance teacher who suspects that one of her students has this problem should contact the American Anorexia Nervosa Association, Inc., 133 Cedar Lane, Teaneck, NJ 07666, or Anorexia Nervosa and Related Eating Disorders, Inc., P.O. Box 5102, Eugene, OR 97405 for information.

4. *Rehabilitation*—This refers to facilitating the return of students to their dance classes following illness or injury. A buddy system accomplishes this reentry with surprising ease and compassion. The dance teacher's role is to monitor the student's transition back to normal functioning and to render both personal and professional assistance when necessary.

5. *Peer counseling*—This is a very effective alternative to professional counseling or faculty advising. This system works particularly well in dance programs because the dance student population is smaller and more unified than in most other disciplines. Senior and graduate dance students can be trained to provide short-term advice and support to younger students. Group counseling can occur within peer groups over matters that concern the dance program as a whole or that group in particular. This is one method of eliciting students' input concerning the issues affecting the operation of their dance program. More importantly, it is a practice that can prevent or defuse personal problems on a one-on-one level and as such exemplifies the pastoral care concept.

6. *Recruitment*—For too long, dance programs have abrogated their responsibility to attract the best possible dance students and have instead relied on the school's admissions office and public relations service to advertise on their behalf. Rarely does anyone representing the arts, let alone dance, participate in college recruiting drives. Scouts for dance are unheard of, and yet the physical qualities and sense of dedication required of dancers are not unlike those of football players. Aggressive recruitment of dance and dance education students is a pastoral care function. Recruiting strategies should be applied on campus as well as on local high school campuses, and dance teachers and administrators should emulate or adapt the practices of the athletic departments in order to increase both the quality and quantity of incoming dancers.

7. *Affirmative Action*—This should be a key pastoral care contact. While dance remains a female-centered field, Affirmative Action compliance is critical to the strength, recognition, and integrity of each dance program. Men in the dance field should be especially aware of the advantages of Affirmative Action since sex discrimination can work both ways (i.e., male dancers are subject to discrimination just as women in male-dominated fields). However, male dancers often get extra opportunities

and are in high demand because of their minority status. Affirmative Action plans, which include Affirmative Action goals and timetables, are available on every campus. Complaint procedures are put into action when students or faculty members allege discriminatory treatment on the basis of age, ancestry, color, handicap, marital status, national origin, race, religion, or sex. Complaints are considered confidential and confidentiality is required of every individual contacted in the course of the investigation.

8. *Learning support services*—Dancers, like athletes, must deftly manage their time to accomplish other kinds of learning. They are possibly more in need of learning support services than other students, as so much of their time is spent in practice, performance, and production. The dance teacher, in a pastoral care capacity, should be able to refer students to services like laboratories, workshops, and tutorials to improve studying, reading, writing, test readiness, problem-solving, memorization, and computation skills. Many dance teachers hold an extra class per week for students to review, catch up, and work on class material.

9. *Sexual harassment awareness*—Recent sexual harassment policies have altered some of the ways teachers relate to their students. Dance teachers and administrators should be fully cognizant of their institution's own policies on what constitutes harassment and how to report incidents.

10. *Legal information*—Dance seems to be one of last professions to become subject to court and legal actions; it is also one of the slowest to avail itself of important legal resources. Judy Chicago (California Lawyers for the Arts, 1987) states: "Artists have traditionally been vulnerable to exploitation, as they often can't afford a lawyer. Even when they can, the language of art is very different from the language of law." Copyright laws, for example, have particular implications for dance choreographers. Whether by default or by design, dancers have for the most part averted many of the legal concerns of other artists. Nevertheless, any pastoral care program for dance should include information on legal issues and ramifications pertinent to the dance profession. The chief issues are as follows:

- Copyrights for choreographies, texts, scores, and costumes; also work-for-hire arrangements, jointly held copyrights, and applying for, renewing, or modifying copyrights
- Contracts between dancers and agents, dance companies and institutions, dance writers and publishers, and dance teachers and school boards, and with film and video companies
- Forms of dance and dance-related businesses (e.g., partnerships, corporations, and proprietorships)

- Income taxes and sales taxes for dance artists, teachers, administrators (e.g., company managers), and technicians
- Insurance claims and small claims court procedures
- Housing and facilities (e.g., residencies, studios, theaters)
- Libel
- Liability

Several states have lawyers for the arts groups, which provide lawyer referrals, dispute resolution services, educational programs, publications, and resource libraries for artists and arts organizations. One such group is California Lawyers for the Arts, which was started in 1974 by lawyers and artists to provide workshops and services to help California artists understand and apply legal concepts to their operations. The group publishes and distributes a series of low-cost art guides designed for practical reading. Titles of interest to the dance profession include *Legislative Masterpieces, Performing Arts Issue With Small Claims Court Guide,* and *Special Performance Issue With Foreign Touring Guide.* These are available from California Lawyers for the Arts, Building C, Room 255, Fort Mason Center, San Francisco, CA 94123.

11. *Program orientation*—Students new to the dance program should be afforded a broad introduction to the facilities, staff, and curriculum. This orientation can be provided by those in charge of pastoral care and can be enhanced by including current dance students as guides and information providers. Some college dance departments conduct orientations during the summer for incoming high school students, while others take advantage of National Dance Week to host an open house for prospective students and their families.
12. *Staff development*—Chapter 7 presented a staff supervision model that included staff and faculty development plans and activities. In the pastoral care context, staff development would emphasize personal development and growth matters, such as job satisfaction, social activities, faculty and staff retreats, updating skills, time-sharing, flexible scheduling, support networks, group dynamics, and time management. Often such matters are left to the program's social chairperson or director; however, a more coordinated approach within the parameters of pastoral care would lead to greater staff harmony and productivity while providing individual growth.
13. *Grievance procedures*—A dance student who feels he or she has been subject to any unfair or improper actions in the pursuit of his or her intellectual, personal, or artistic growth should be able to seek redress through filing an appeal or grievance. Each institution handles student grievances within a framework of approved legal policy and procedures.

Table 8.2 summarizes the appropriate channels to be utilized by a dance student at the College of San Mateo, CA, who wishes to appeal an action or decision.

Those in charge of pastoral care should encourage informal approaches in the early stages of the grievance procedure. The dance student should attempt to resolve the dispute directly and informally with the appropriate faculty member in a timely manner. If the disagreement is not resolved at this juncture, then the student may initiate a formal appeal. The pastoral care advisor should be equipped to guide the student through this process or to refer the student to the legitimate grievance office on campus. If the grievance procedure is prolonged or requires resolution beyond the college level, the student's advisor should provide effective professional and emotional support.

Table 8.2   Channels of Appeal Available to Students

Subject	Source of initial decision/action	Appropriate channel of appeal
Academic grievances	Instructor Division director	Division director Vice president
Academic probation/ dismissal	College policy	Standards committee
Admissions	Director of admissions	Dean of student services
Attendance	Instructor	Attendance committee
Payment/refund of fees & nonresident tuition	Director of admissions	Dean of student services
Discipline	Dean of student services	President
Financial aid	Financial aid officer	Director of admissions
Parking citations & security matters	Security staff Chief of campus security	Chief of campus security Dean of student services
Residency determination	Director of admissions	Dean of student services
Student records	Director of admissions	Dean of student services
Time, place, & manner	College policy	Dean of student services
Waiver of academic requirements	College policy	Academic review committee
Withdrawal (late)	College policy	Standards committee
Matters not listed above	College policy/staff	Dean of student services

14. *Volunteer opportunities*—To gain hands-on experience in dance education, nothing is more practical and valuable than volunteer assignments in schools, youth agencies, and community institutions. These assignments range from babysitting to program planning, and they involve individuals from preschoolers to the elderly. Both students and teachers can benefit from these experiences. Indeed, teachers who train and supervise student dance teachers should spend time in schools and other places where dance is taught and performed. These volunteer opportunities help hone their teaching skills and also expose teachers to the continually evolving younger generation; educators who are not in touch with schools lack credibility and currentness. More information on volunteer organizations can be found in the *I CAN Volunteer Development Workbook*, available from the National Center for Citizen Involvement's Volunteer Readership Service, Box 1807, Boulder, CO 80306. An *I CAN Advisor's Manual* and *I CAN Administrative Guidelines* are also available from the same service for dance teachers wishing to recruit and train volunteers from among their dance students. Contact the nearest Volunteer Action Committee (VAC), which is an organization with nationwide affiliations, to enlist help in matching volunteers with the non-profit agencies. Volunteerism is not only a way of paying one's dues; it is a way of actively demonstrating interest and involvement in a worthy cause.

15. *Child care*—''There is a big difference between what child care in this country should be and what it has been forced to become because it lacks social support'' (Boston Women's Health Book Collective, 1984, p. 413). These days, most dance students have witnessed the presence of a stroller in class at one time or another. Child care provision at schools and on campuses leaves much to be desired, and until it becomes socially acceptable for mothers to work and study, child care will be inadequate. Federal and state financial support for child care has been limited largely because budget committee members continue to believe that families should be kept intact and that home care is the best care. For dance students and teachers, dropping out of the job and performance markets for several years can have economic and professional costs. Thus pastoral care givers should lobby for ''thoughtfully-designed, well-equipped, well-staffed child care centers'' (Boston Women's Health Book Collective, 1984, p. 413). A resource book to have on hand is *Family Daycare: A Practical Guide for Parents, Caregivers and Professionals* by Alice H. Collins and Eunice L. Watson (Beacon Press, Boston, 1976). For a political and historical perspective of child care in this country, read *Who's Minding the Children: The History and Politics of Day Care in America* by Margaret O'Brian Steinfels (Simon & Schuster, New York, 1973).

16. *Special population services*—Dance students and colleagues who fall within a special population should receive special attention. Special in this context includes persons with chronic, genetic, or congenital conditions that affect the way they move and behave. People take dance classes who have a wide variety of disabilities, from heart conditions and cancer to multiple sclerosis and sickle cell anemia. Pastoral care must be flexible and multilateral, and must consider dance facilities, services, adaptive dance, wheelchair access, medications, transportation, medical releases, liability, and scheduling. Texts and articles by dance therapists are among the best resources. So too are materials available at the disabled students' office found on most campuses.

17. *Opportunity for studying abroad*—The lure of overseas travel haunts most people who work in the arts, and dance students and teachers are no exceptions. Dance students can benefit from an international perspective that reflects the world in realistic artistic and educational terms. Many institutions already have ties to other countries, and several have developed outstanding international programs. California Polytechnic State University offers a quarter-long London study program that is almost entirely devoted to the arts. It draws students from all majors, and the courses are enriched by visiting lecturers and artists from British institutions. International student exchanges can be sought or arranged by dance teachers and administrators, often as a result of admitting foreign students into their college dance program. International dance is an area of enrichment and expansion, for the dance students who take part and for the dance program as a whole, as international study transforms narrow regional perspectives into global ones. A reference work to consider is *International Education: A Directory of Resource Materials on Comparative Education and Study in Another Country* by Lily von Klemperer (Garrett Park Press, Garrett Park, MD, 1973).

18. *Cooperative education, work experience, and internships*—In dance education, as in any other professional field, there is no substitute for hands-on training. Student teachers in dance are required to complete preservice teaching assignments and do so in elementary and secondary schools under the supervision of their faculty advisor and a cooperative teacher in the school. These student teaching assignments earn academic credit and constitute a significant component of the teaching credential. These are model experiences with respect to pastoral care and are administered according to academic policies. I feel however, that all dance students should have work experience related to their career interests and that providing these opportunities is a pastoral care mission. Help can be found in the local or university library in the form of directories; for example, *Directory of Internships, Work Experience Programs,* and *On-The-Job-Training Opportunities* (Ready

Reference Press, Box 5169, Santa Monica, CA 90405). Also check your institution's cooperative education program, which allows students to earn credit for learning on the job. Cooperative education students may be employed on a paid or volunteer bàsis. Cooperative education experiences are particularly suited to dance students who wish to learn nonteaching or nonperforming skills, such as stage design, dance journalism, arts administration, or costuming. In this manner dance students can gain insight into the relevance of their coursework as they work with experts in the field and establish professional contacts.

19. *AIDS education*—AIDS (Acquired Immune Deficiency Syndrome) is a fatal disease with no known cure which primarily affects male homosexuals, intravenous drug users, hemophiliacs, and the babies of female drug users. Its effects are seen most dramatically and severely amongst male dancers, teachers, and choreographers. The epidemic's effects on the dance field, which are largely undocumented, are regarded within the profession itself as utterly devastating. Soozie Childers, Las Vegas choreographer and director of the Foster City Dance Theatre, maintains that the ranks of talented male dancers in the entertainment industry and in well-known ballet companies is being drastically reduced because of AIDS. Education is the only way to prevent further spread of the disease. An effective way to stem this epidemic is to educate the youth about AIDS and to intervene when there is reason to believe that students are at risk. More information may be obtained by contacting *The National AIDS Network* (2033 M Street NW, Suite 800, Washington, DC 20036).

Conclusions

The concept of pastoral care programming with support services for dance teaching and learning institutions may seem novel at first; in reality it is already practiced by most dance teachers. It is the hidden curriculum for successful living and working. Teachers will no doubt find many familiar items in this chapter, as they have overtly and tacitly incorporated pastoral care into their student advising responsibilities for some time. Chapter 9 discusses a more revolutionary concept—computer technology and its impact on dance.

Key Terms

Academic—relating to studies that are liberal or classical rather than technical or vocational

Affirmative Action—action taken to provide equal opportunity for minority groups

Career guidance—direction and support services related to entering occupations or professions

Contracts—agreements between two or more parties that are documented and enforceable

Cooperative education—education that involves an association of people and businesses for mutual benefit

Copyright laws—legal rights given to artists, authors, and publishers to exclusive publication, production, or sale of a literary, dramatic, artistic, or musical work

Eating disorders—problems associated with eating (e.g., overeating, undereating, anorexia, and bulima)

Grievance procedures—approved ways to deal with complaints, protests, and unjust actions

Health maintenance—the ongoing preservation of optimal health

Injury prevention—prevention of damage or impairment to the body

Inreach activities—activities that provide services to and within a specified group or program

Interdisciplinary programs—programs that combine more than one field of academic study

International education—education that extends across the boundaries of two or more countries

Learning support—services and assistance to increase ability to master knowledge and skills

Orientation—adjustment or adaption to a new environment by means of introductory instructions and assistance

Outreach activities—activities that provide services beyond conventional program limits

Pastoral—relating to the physical and emotional welfare or guidance of persons in one's care

Placement service—the business of finding jobs or other positions for applicants

Recruitment—active search for students or applicants

Rehabilitation—process of restoring to useful activity through education and therapy

Sexual harassment—persecution by sexual annoyances, threats, or demands

Special populations—groups of people who fall outside the usual or common

Staff development—opportunities that provide for the professional and personal growth of employees

Stress management—systematic control of mentally or emotionally disruptive influences

Substance abuse—improper or injurious use of drugs

Volunteerism—practice of being a volunteer or using volunteers in community service work

Student Activities and Assignments

1. Locate your institution's policy documentation on the following pastoral care issues:
   - Affirmative Action
   - Grievances
   - Sexual harassment
   - Copyright
   - Equal Employment Opportunity
2. In collaboration with your institution's cooperative education office, prepare a list of potential dance and dance-related work opportunities available on campus and in the community.
3. Conduct a dance injury survey among dance students in your school or program. Consider incidence, duration, and type of injury. Tabulate your results and make recommendations for an injury prevention workshop or an ongoing program.

Further Reading

Bolles, R.N. (1983). *What color is your parachute? A practical manual for job-hunters and career-changers*. Berkeley, CA: Ten Speed Press.

The Boston Women's Health Book Collective. (1985). *The new our bodies, ourselves*. New York: Simon & Schuster.

Jacob, E. (1981). *A guide for the dancer you can be*. Reading, MA: Addison-Wesley.

Minton, S. (1987). Dance dynamics: Avoiding dance injuries. *Journal of Physical Education, Recreation and Dance,* **58**(5), 29-60.

Chapter 9
Technology and Dance

The technological revolution has not yet produced a civilization of programmed robots and is unlikely to do so. It has, however, infiltrated almost every aspect of our lives, making human relations more precious and important than ever before. In schools and colleges, the overwhelming availability of information and options is producing a generation of bewildered students not unlike the alienated students of the 1960s. The difference is that instead of having too few choices, today's students have too many; our era is rightly called the era of overchoice. This chapter discusses changes resulting from the rise of technology.

The Rise of Dance Technology

The field of dance technology has grown rapidly and diversified remarkably since the first symposium on computers and dance convened in

1981 at the annual National Dance Association conference in Anaheim, California, and was followed by publication of a monograph featuring selected articles on the subject (Gray, 1983b). Work in this field has not been without frustrations; in some instances technology has far surpassed the ability of dance researchers to harness it (e.g., laser technology) while in other areas technology lags behind the far-reaching ideas and concepts of those working in these fields (e.g., dance notation and text analysis). However, cooperation and integration always prevail in dance technology research. The dance profession is inextricably tied to the new information technologies through curiosity and interdependence: curiosity because it leads to experimentation, innovation, risk taking, and problem solving, and interdependence because technicians (e.g., systems analysts, programmers, engineers, mathematicians, and anatomists) cannot proceed far without input from conceptualists (e.g., choreographers, notators, historians, and behaviorists). The advantage of such interdependence (which is rarely found in other disciplines) is illustrated by Eddie Dombrower's DOM system (Dombrower, 1984), a computerized graphic notation system that combines artistic merit and mathematical prowess. Dance educators will benefit from recognizing and following the trends, directions, and implications of the Information Age technologies.

This chapter represents an effort to update and expand upon computer applications that pertain to dance education, which have been developed continually since the late 1970s. The chapter also looks beyond current computer technology to lasers, holography, digitizing, robotics, and artificial intelligence. The chapter concludes with future directions for dance education research in the Information Age (or the Third Wave, as Alvin Toffler [1981] calls it) and with an assurance that dance educators and computer scientists have nothing to fear from each other. Indeed, in the future little may distinguish the two.

Background

The first attempt to combine computer technology and dance occurred in the 1960s at the University of Pittsburgh, when Jean Beaman used a computer to design choreography. In the 1970s several researchers devised techniques to computerize Labanotation—the symbolic scoring system for recording dances (see Figure 9.1); these techniques have since been expanded to include editing, analyzing, and complex manipulation (Sealy, 1982).

Computerized notation systems later incorporated graphics components and sound synthesizers so notated dances could be visualized on the computer's monitor as well as be accompanied by computer-generated music. The consequent implications for archival research and experimental choreography

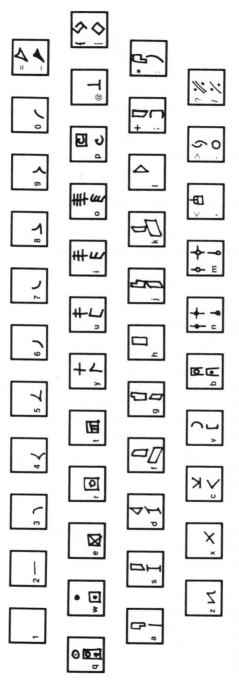

Figure 9.1. Labanotation key assignments. *Note.* From "Dance in Computer Technology" by Judith A. Gray, 1984, *Interchange,* 15(4), p. 15-25. Copyright 1984 by The Ontario Institute for Studies in Education, Toronto, Canada. Reprinted by permission.

were boundless. Also during the 1970s researchers made advances in computerized body modeling for dance (see Figure 9.2), beginning with simple stick figure graphics and culminating in Smoliar's "Sausageman" (Weber & Smoliar, 1978) and Emmett's "Bubbleman" (1978). Soon after, dance audiences were treated to an exquisite, lithesome computerized dancer comprised of light rods in Twyla Tharp's 1983 video choreography "Catherine Wheel" (Allen, 1983). Recently, music videos have frequently featured dancer digitizations.

Also in the 1970s, attempts were made to monitor and analyze human motion using computers and film. These efforts were concentrated in dance kinesiology (Shea, 1981) and goniometrics (Lessard, 1980), and they paved the way for the less cumbersome and more sophisticated systems of the 1980s.

In the late 1970s and early 1980s, dance educators became increasingly intrigued with the potential of computerization and attempted to develop computer-aided instruction (CAI) programs for dance (Gray & Degan, 1983) and to record and analyze dance teacher behaviors (Gray, 1983a). Buff Brennan (1985) at the University of Wisconsin-Madison designed a computer-aided method for analyzing dance movement based on the Labananalysis system; she introduced this method to the dance profession at the 1987 National Dance Association conference. Meanwhile at Stanford University, Margot Apostolos (1984, 1987) tested a robotic arm's capability for aesthetic movement and produced videotapes of the spectacular results. Other innovations of the early 1980s include a graphics editor for Benesh movement notation (Singh, Beatty, Booth, & Ryman, 1983), more sophisticated computerized programs for Labanotation (Sealy, 1982), dance image digitization (Pope & Gray, 1983), and a wide range of business, bibliographic, and administrative software for dance. Dance technology is a young field; much more is left to be achieved and more skeptics have to be won over. The number of dance technologists in the 1980s is under 50, yet they are making their presence felt in education, computer science, the media, and information technology.

Computer Use

The computer is most often used for notation, choreography, and dance administration; most dance educators have resisted using computer-based instruction approaches, despite the following advantages:

- Individual help is available to a student who might otherwise be ignored.
- By being able to work at their own paces, children of different capacities are not restricted in their learning curves.
- The computer is impartial, patient, and objective, and the student can receive immediate feedback (Sanders, 1985).

None of these advantages applies in a technique class; however, the technology should not be rejected because of narrow definitions of dance content and instructional methodology and because of teacher resistance.

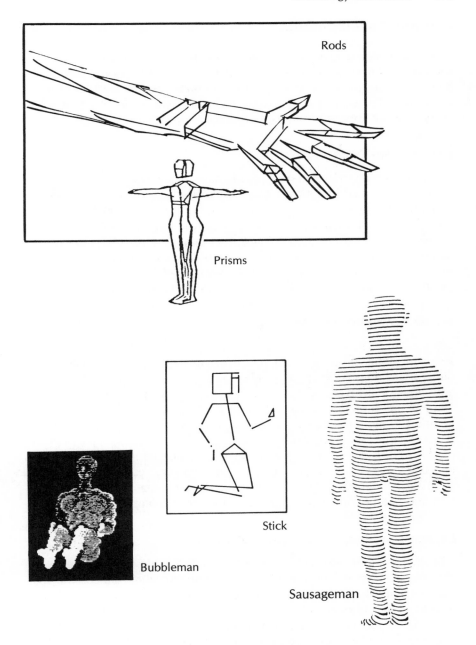

Figure 9.2. Computerized body models for dance. *Note.* From "Dance in Computer Technology" by Judith A. Gray, 1984, *Interchange*, **15**(4), p. 15-25. Copyright 1984 by The Ontario Institute for Studies in Education, Toronto, Canada. Reprinted by permission.

Current Developments

Several university dance departments in the U.S. and abroad support and sponsor projects that combine the art of dance with the science of computers. The dance scholars and technicians involved in these projects spearhead dance research that is on the cutting edge of technology. Following is a list of current exploratory innovations in dance technology.

Dance Video Digitizing

This process is an extension of standard image digitizing procedures; still pictures are converted into movable manipulated images that provide another dimension to the dance performance environment. Soon, computerized video images and scenes will be adapted to the cyclorama for a more realistic or surrealistic effect. These digital images are helpful in dance instruction because they allow teachers to graphically arrest, analyze, and manipulate the phrases and dances of students. Several dances can be viewed at one time, or one dance can be viewed from every possible vantage point.

LOGO 3-Dimensional Modeling

Dianne Petty (1985) at UCLA has created a human model of a dancer on the geometric design processor—an interactive graphics system for modeling three-dimensional objects. She photographed a series of computer-generated poses and subsequently blended these images with choreography, music, costumes, and lighting to produce a unique dance performance. Her project began as an effort to design dance movement on a computer before instructing live dancers. Petty asked herself these questions: "What choreographic development could be solved more readily on a computer before putting it on live dancers? What possibilities of blending computer graphics and live dance had been already explored?" (p. 5). Her successful combination of computerization and live performance is now available on videotape.

Lasers, Opto-Electronics, and Holography

Holography was invented over two decades ago and almost immediately became an artistic tool. Holographic techniques produce three-dimensional light patterns that change perspective and color as viewers alter position or move around them. Although holograms of dances and dancers have not yet been created, it is possible to imagine the likely effects. Computer-generated holograms exist of other structured situations, notably in the fields of architecture, engineering, and medicine. The implications for teaching dance composition with holographic aids are exciting.

Data Banks and Information Networks

Two major electronic dance resources were recently developed in this country. The first was initiated by Pat Rowe (1985) at New York University and was designed to provide ready access to a wide variety of dance information. The host information network, called SOURCE, enables dancers, teachers, administrators, and the general public to tap into the latest data on events, publications, reports, jobs, and funding. The second resource is aimed primarily at the dance researcher and will ultimately provide a comprehensive bibliographic data base (Ruyter, 1986). This project, directed by Nancy Ruyter at UCLA, will eventually render laborious library and archival searches obsolete. Both of these resources will be invaluable to dance teachers and researchers.

Motion Detectors

At Tufts University, a motion detector originally used in science laboratories has been adapted for use in dance instruction and performance. Alice Trexler and Ronald Thornton (1986), working with dance composition students, have produced computer-generated graphs of movement paths and patterns. "The motion detector sends out short pulses of high frequency and detects the echo (much the way a bat locates objects in the dark). By using a microcomputer to measure the time between the transmitted and received pulse, it is possible to calculate the position and velocity of the body and to display this information on a computer monitor" (p. 1). They contend that these displays will not only facilitate cross-disciplinary collaborations but will also act as aesthetic catalysts for both dancers and choreographers. Teachers of dance will utilize the graphed patterns of student movements to conduct evaluations and critiques.

Robot Choreography

While at Stanford University, Margo Apostolos found that users of robotic aids who understood the aids' potential range of aesthetic movement qualities had enhanced attitudes towards these devices (Curtis & Apostolos, 1986). Apostolos has since developed a body of work in robot choreography that demonstrates the expressive potential of the computer-driven machines. Apostolos (1987) has incorporated computer technological terms into her teaching and has created dances for students and a large robot.

Interactive Compact Discs

Compact disc-interactive (CD-I) is a proposed standard for a new type of education/entertainment device that has already been used successfully in a social studies classroom (Raleigh, 1986). CD-I capacity adds a visual dimension to the high-quality sound now available with audio compact discs and the text and graphics storage of compact disc-read only memory (CD-ROM). For dance this means that the works of a single choreographer could be contained on a single disc along with a comprehensive biography, the notated music and dance scores, and critical reviews and analyses. This material could form part of a media encyclopedia much like the current comprehensive reference data base on the Cray computer. This technology has obvious advantages for the teaching of dance history and dance ethnology. Dance technique teachers and their students will also find this effective for storing other types of information.

Future Developments

Prospects for dance education research in the Information Age depend on the level of computer literacy among dance teachers and their students. The new technologies can no longer be accepted or rejected by dance or any of the other arts. Technology influences not only the artistic or academic product but also the process—the means by which dance artists and scholars gain their ends.

According to Kruger (1983), "We are shaped as much by our tools as our tools are shaped by us. More and more we are integrating ourselves and our machines" (p. 187). Possibly, the best way to integrate the computer and the arts is to focus on the aesthetic process rather than on the production of a finished work of art. Dance education should emphasize the alternatives that the computer can provide (Kruger, 1983). More on these exploratory research constructs and projections follows.

Computerized Dance Environments

In a computer-controlled dance environment, a new kind of dance with far-reaching implications for dance education can evolve. Dance teachers and their students will be able to build and test a new range of choreographic and production resources. Instead of the dancer responding to an accompanying sound, the reverse could apply. The dancer will orchestrate the music, lights, and backdrops using only her movements. Ed Tannenbaum (1984) in San Francisco has already produced demonstration performances in which a dancer moves in relation to his or her own digitized video image. Entire dances are choreographed interactively with the computer, and the effect is one of artful distortion, complicity, and enhancement of reality. In these performances the dancer's environment ultimately becomes an extension of the performer. Moreover, computerized dance environments could allow the dance audience to consciously or unconsciously influence the environment by means of computer controls by their seats.

Holography

Rear screen video projections or monitorized cycloramas will allow multiple images of dancers, ranging from lifelike images to endless digitized variations and modifications. With the development of holography it may soon be possible to create dances with no real people performing. Three-dimensional human body simulations that have been generated and manipulated by computer will appear in the dance environment unhampered by the laws of motion and gravity. These holographic dancers could even be choreographed to interact with live dancers, challenging the audience to distinguish the real from the non-real. Non-real images could also include scenery, props, stage boundaries, and other production considerations. Traditional relationships between audience and performer, between the environment and the performer, and between the performers themselves will be eroded and a new set of expectations and responsibilities will emerge. Dance educators can be catalysts in this trend.

Illusionism

The new technologies will generate the ultimate illusion for dance, *Illusionism*, which is defined as realism protracted to a point where the real and the non-real are indistinguishable. Illusionism will be a movement style that aims to confuse the observer as to whether what is seen is object or artifice (Frude, 1983). Computer technology has the ability to create such dilemmas in profusion and in doing so will also create audiences who will enjoy and intimately involve themselves in the artistic ambiguity. A performance lacking traditional relationships becomes an automated happening, a theatrical situation in which the participants are responsible for their own experience (Kruger, 1983). Artificial reality, therefore, may well become the norm.

Future Directions for Dance and Dance Education

Computerized dance environments, holography, and illusionism will extend traditional pedagogical boundaries and by doing so will more clearly unite the art of technology with the art of education. Dance will thus be viewed in the context of a technological arena, from which it can derive educational insights and benefits. This view of dance, (which may seem farfetched at this point) allows us to conjure up a future in which almost everything is possible. Some of the possibilities of interest to dance educators are as follows:

- Humanistic (humanoid?) computerized dancer models
- Voice input that instructs computers to alter or create dance images
- Choreographic decision making by specially designed artificial intelligence software

- Holographic images of dancers and the evolution of illusionism as a dance style
- Patterns of light and spatial configurations that oscillate around or in response to dancers
- Video sensory systems that accurately record and analyze dance movements
- Pseudo dance in which the human images are capable of cartoon-like articulations
- Concept and skill instruction for dance using sophisticated CAI software and interactive simulations
- Expert systems for dance and dance education whereby vast amounts of dance information and heuristics are compiled to produce solutions for aesthetic and educational problems
- Dance knowledge engineers who assist the profession by managing and integrating dance's computer software needs

Conclusions

The continued interplay of dance and the new technologies will most certainly change the face and perception of dance. The dance scholar and educator will have more information than ever before, and moreover it will be highly managed, accessible, and disseminated. The relationship between the dance performer and the environment will be limited only by the imagination of the choreographer. Audiences will be redefined, and dance literacy will employ a distinctly modified vocabulary. Dance teachers will have on-line access to teaching software and teaching aids. Technology will also bring associated problems, including funding and time considerations, obtrusiveness of equipment, untrained or computer-illiterate personnel, lack of interface devices, memory limitations, and above all, the philosophic and practical difficulties of reproducing, preserving, and interpreting the aesthetic of dance. The inclusion of computer courses within dance curricula clearly becomes imperative.

The new age will demand greater collaboration and communication. Dance professionals will work with computer scientists, programmers, technicians, and engineers. We will be responsible for providing the conceptual and artistic input, which will in turn require processing and management expertise. The more that dance educators know about computers, the easier it will be to make decisions regarding the use and misuse of the new technologies and their inevitable impact on students and on the field. These are challenges that dance educators will have to face. As we have learned from past technological revolutions, artists and teachers who can unite the power and promise of the new technology with the needs and parameters of their profession will be the winners.

Key Terms

Artificial intelligence—a branch of computer science that uses computers to solve problems that appear to require human imagination or intelligence

Body modeling—constructing or shaping of the human body to scale

Computer-aided instruction—the acquisition of knowledge and skills with the assistance of a computer

Dance technology—the application of computer and information science to the field of dance

Data—facts; the raw material of information

Data base—a collection of data arranged for ease and speed of retrieval, as by a computer

Data bank—an organization or structure that builds, stores, and maintains a data base

Graphics—the making of drawings and diagrams with the rules of mathematics

Holography—the technique of producing images by using lasers to record on a photographic plate the diffraction pattern from which a three-dimensional pattern or image can be projected

Image digitizing—reproducing a likeness of an object in digits for computer use

Information network—a chain or system of interconnected electric components and circuitry relaying information

Information technology—the application of computer technology to the gathering, manipulation, classification, storage, and retrieval of recorded knowledge

Laser—device that converts radiation of mixed frequencies into one highly amplified and coherent light beam

Robot—a mechanical device that resembles a human being and is operated automatically or by remote control

Student Activities and Assignments

1. Identify the computer system you use at home, work, or school. What applications or software would you like to see designed in order to improve your dance instructional program?
2. Discuss arguments for and against including computer science courses as part of graduation or promotion requirements for dance students and teachers.
3. Investigate the computerization of other arts, such as music, theater, and the fine arts. Prepare a paper that discusses the results of your investigation.

4. "Optimistic forecasters believe that computer usage will result in greater freedom and individuality and a more human and personalized society." State whether you agree with this statement, and defend your response with reference to dance as art and dance as an educational force.

Further Reading

Caulfield, J.H. (1984). The wonders of holography. *National Geographic*, **165**(3), 365-367.
Frude, N. (1983). *The intimate machine*. London: Century.
Gray, J.A. (1989). *Dance technology: Current applications and future trends.* Reston, VA: American Alliance for Health, Physical Education, Recreation and Dance.
Kruger, M.W. (1983). *Artificial reality*. Menlo Park, CA: Addison-Wesley.

Chapter 10

Epilogue

The teaching and learning of dance are preparations for the future. "All education springs from some image of the future," maintains Alvin Toffler (1974). "If the image of the future held by a society is grossly inaccurate, its education system will betray its youth" (p. 3). Unless teachers more fully comprehend the future for which they prepare their students, they may unwittingly misinform, distract, or do long-term damage to their charges. Unfortunately, most schools and colleges base their teaching and learning philosophies on the assumption that the future will be similar to the present, despite evidence to the contrary. A complacency exists in dance education today, as it does in other teaching disciplines. According to Toffler (1984), our institutions of learning, whether they be schools, studios, gyms, or community centers, comprise an archaic educational system rooted in an industrial or factory model of knowledge and skill acquisition. In this model, dance learning is based on the principles of standardization, specialization, uniformity, and conformity. Dance students typically learn in rows, practice uniformly prescribed steps, and are encouraged to specialize in a single dance form. They are evaluated according to a rigid set of criteria—alignment, timing, accurate execution, and level of flexibility, much like a gymnast or a machine.

Developing an alternative to this educational system requires reform of dramatic proportions. The new model must embrace the principles of diversity, individualization, cognition, problem solving, exploration, customization, and integration. These are the compelling factors of Toffler's *third wave theory* (1984), wherein the third wave is an era of unprecedented technological development characterized by computerization and social change. Dance education in particular lends itself to this theory, especially if it is conceptualized and analyzed in terms of information theory. This reconceptualization shifts the emphasis from explaining dance learning in behavioristic terms to explaining learning in cognitive terms. The management of dance information thus becomes more important to the critical concerns in dance education: not only what is being learned, but how it is learned.

The idea that knowledge is power in dance education management is now suspect. To achieve respect and leadership in the field today, dance educators must possess knowledge about dance knowledge. In other words, knowing only hard facts and figures is not only insufficient, but is impossible considering today's information explosion. While Margaret H'Doubler and others ably demonstrated their knowledge about dance teaching and learning as it related to the then-contemporary education theory, their approach is now no longer appropriate nor viable as dance education continues to evolve historically, cognitively, and technologically. To increase knowledge about dance knowledge itself, educators must employ information science analogies and cognitive science explanations to all aspects of the dance teaching and learning processes. The dance learners of tomorrow will possess highly organized information, greater imagination, and unimaginable resources in the quest to know dance. Mind work will become equally as important as body work, perhaps even more so. The dance art will expand along cognitive and sentient matrices. The role of dance education in this shift toward a third wave information technology philosophy is critical to the future of the art form.

We are at a crucial moment in dance education history, a moment at the heart of the change between traditional behavioristic learning models and the newer information-based cognitive models of education. Dance education will become more complex, more diverse, and more prone to changes in direction and pace, requiring involvement of teachers and students in decision making. The process will become more participatory and symbiotic. Ensuing generations of dance students will inevitably bring more and more information into the dance learning environment. The question will be how to manage the knowledge base in order to produce the best and most diversified dancers, choreographers, theorists, audiences, and technologists. Schools and universities will not likely be the sole providers of the necessary momentum, as innovations and preparations for dance in the future are happening outside of the schools and colleges. Different branches of the dance education field must collaborate if dance education is to retain its strength of purpose.

Our educational system is in trouble; according to Jerry Pournelle (1986), "even if we fix the school system to do what it's supposed to do now, it will still be inadequate for the world we foresee." (p. 23). The curriculum in the schools today is replete with procedures geared to teaching facts and basic skills. It exemplifies the worst kind of retrenchment and failure to confront reality, as factual knowledge will in the future be redundant or useless. Pournelle adds that in the new information society, "the real power will come from knowing what questions to ask since anyone can get answers" (p. 23). Problem solving as a teaching/learning strategy will thus emphasize knowing what problems to present, rather than the possible resolutions. As schools are primarily geared to providing answers only, enlightened parents will be more inclined to look elsewhere for education providers. Arts and the new technologies, which are already in the business of questions and questioning, will play an increasingly large role in education of and for the future. Dance educators can clearly play a vital part. Dance and its information base can be part of the planning and design of tomorrow's schools—a task of immense proportions and complexity (see Figure 10.1). States Toffler (1974), "Thus to

Figure 10.1. The teaching and learning of dance is preparation for the future. *Note.* Photo courtesy of Brent Nicastro.

design educational systems for tomorrow (or even for today) we need . . . something far more complicated: sets of images of successive and alternative futures, each one tentative and different from the next'' (p. 15). The implications for dance education inquiry and research are momentous.

This book's discussion of the teaching and learning of dance should help pave the way for futurist thinking about dance education and about dance as education. The future is here; the future is now. As dance educators we can determine its quality and direction.

Further Reading

Toffler, A. (1974). The psychology of the future. In A. Toffler (Ed.), *Learning for tomorrow: The role of the future in education* (pp. 3-18). New York: Random House.

Bibliography

A nation at risk: The imperative for educational reform. A report to the nation and the Secretary of Education. (1983). Washington, DC: United States Department of Education.

Acheson, K.A., & Gall, M.D. (1980). *Techniques in the clinical supervision of teachers.* New York: Longman.

Adams, R.S., & Biddle, B.J. (1970). *Realities of teaching: Explorations with videotape.* New York: Holt.

Ainsworth, M.D.S., & Wittig, B.A. (1969). Attachment and exploratory behavior of one-year-olds in a strange situation. In B.M. Foss (Ed.), *Determinants of infant behavior* (Vol. 4) (pp. 111-136). London: Methuen.

Alaska Department of Education. (1985). *Elementary fine arts: Alaska curriculum guide.* Juneau, AK: Author.

Allen, R. (1983). The bionic dancer. *Journal of Physical Education, Recreation and Dance,* **54**(9), 38-39.

Anderson, H.J., & Barrette, G.T. (Eds.) (1978). *What's going on in gym: Descriptive studies of physical education classes* (Monograph 1). Newtown, CT: Motor Skills: Theory into Practice.

Apostolos, M. (1984, April). *Robotic arm choreography.* Paper presented at the annual conference of the American Association of Health, Physical Education, Recreation and Dance, Anaheim, CA.

Apostolos, M. (1987, October). *Mars Suite: A performance of human and robotic dancers.* Paper presented at the Congress on Research in Dance annual conference, New York University, NY.

Arbeau, T. (1967). *Orchesography*. (M. Steward Evans, Trans.; J. Sutton, Ed.). New York: Dover. (Original work published 1589)

Asher, H.B. (1983). *Causal modeling*. Beverly Hills, CA: Sage.

Barrette, K.R. (1977). Studying teaching—A means for becoming a more effective teacher. In B. Logsdon (Ed.), *Physical education for children: A focus on the teaching process* (pp. 271-272). Philadelphia: Lea & Febiger.

Bergfield, J.A. (1982). Medical problems in ballet. *The Physician and Sportsmedicine*, **10**(3), 103.

Bernard, H.W. (1965). *Psychology of learning and teaching*. New York: McGraw-Hill.

Blalock, H.M. (1964). *Causal inferences and measurement in non-experimental research*. Chapel Hill: University of North Carolina Press.

Blalock, H.M. (1982). *Conceptualization and measurement in the social sciences*. Beverly Hills, CA: Sage.

Borger, R., & Seaborne, A.E.M. (1982). *The psychology of learning*. Bungay, Suffolk, England: Chaucer Press.

Boston Women's Health Book Collective. (1985). *The new our bodies, ourselves*. New York: Simon & Schuster.

Brauer, L. (1975). Teaching approaches in modern dance (Doctoral dissertation, Rutgers University). *Dissertation Abstracts International*, **36A**, 4120.

Brennan, M.A. (1982). *A computerized methodology for recording and analyzing movement element combinations*. Unpublished manuscript, University of Wisconsin-Madison.

Bruner, J.S. (1966). *Toward a theory of instruction*. Cambridge, MA: Harvard University Press.

Buehler, R.E., & Richmond, J.F. (1963). Inter-personal communication behavior analysis: A research method. *Journal of Communication*, **13**, 146-153.

California Lawyers for the Arts. (1987). (Brochure available from California Lawyers for the Arts, Building C, Room 255, Fort Mason Center, San Francisco, CA 94123)

Carver, V.M., & Frangione, D. (1985, April). Choreographic evaluation. *Dance Teacher Now*, pp. 17-24.

Catelli, L.A. (1979). Verbal and non-verbal moves in teaching: A descriptive system for the analysis of teaching physical education (Doctoral dissertation, Columbia University). *Dissertation Abstracts International*, **40A**, 19, 40, 147-A.

Chalif, L. (1916). *The Chalif text book of dancing*. New York: Isaac Goldman.

Combest, S., Weise, C., & Caton, I. (1986, March). Higher education: Preparing dancers for more than one career. *Journal of Physical Education, Recreation and Dance*, **57**(3), 73-77.

Crawley, J.N., Szaras, G.T., Pryor, C.R., Creveling, C., & Bernard, B.K. (1982). Development and evaluation of a computer-automated color T.V. tracking system for automatic recording of the social and exploratory behavior of small animals. *Journal of Neuroscience*, **5**, 234-247.

Curtis, G., & Apostolos, M. (1986). *The role of choreographic exploration in the design of the robotic aid*. Paper presented at the Arts and Technology Symposium, Connecticut College, New London, CT.

De Cecco, J. (1968). *The psychology of learning and instruction: Educational psychology*. Englewood Cliffs, NJ: Prentice Hall.

Dombrower, E. (1984). *The DOM system*. Paper presented at the annual conference of the American Association for Health, Physical Education, Recreation and Dance, Anaheim, CA.

Dossey, L. (1982). *Space, time and medicine*. Boulder, CO: Shambhala.

Dunkin, M.J., & Biddle, B.J. (1974). *The study of teaching*. New York: Holt, Rinehart, & Winston.

Eisner, E. (1986). The role of the arts in cognition and curriculum. *Journal of Art & Design Education*, **5**(1&2), 57-67.

Ellfeldt, L. (1967). *A primer for choreographers*. Palo Alto, CA: Mayfield.

Emmett, C. (1978). *The development of computer animation methods for body animation* (Rep. 194/1). London: Department of Design Research, Royal College of Art.

Ensign, C. (1976). An examination of the effects of range, frequency, and duration of movement on rhythmic synchronization (Doctoral dissertation, University of Wisconsin, Madison). *Dissertation Abstracts International*, **37A**, 6543.

Freedman, J.O. (1987). The tendency toward specialization has had fragmenting consequences. *Chronicle of Higher Education*, **33**(48), 47.

Frude, N. (1983). *The intimate machine*. London: Century Publishing.

Galloway, C.M. (1970). *Teaching is communicating: Non-verbal language in the classroom* (Association for Teaching, Bulletin No. 29). Washington, DC: National Endowment for the Arts.

Gray, J.A. (1983a). The dance teacher: A computerized behavioral profile. *Journal of Physical Education, Recreation and Dance*, **54**(9), 34-35.

Gray, J.A. (1983b). A computer-aided investigation of the location behaviors of dance teachers. In S.K. Burton & D.B. Short (Eds.), *Sixth Annual International Conference on Computers and the Humanities* (pp. 225-232). Maryland: Computer Science Press.

Gray, J.A. (1984a). A computerized technique for recording and analyzing teacher mobility. *Journal of Educational Studies*, **10**(2), 23-30.

Gray, J.A. (1984b). A conceptual framework for the study of dance teaching. *Quest*, **36**, 153-163.

Gray, J.A. (1986). Teaching children's dance: Behaviors, strategies, and learning time. In *Dance: The New Zealand experience* (pp. 85-90). Auckland, New Zealand: Auckland Teachers College.

Gray, J.A., & Degen, T. (1983). *CODANS: Computer dance composition* [Computer program]. University of Wisconsin, Madison. (Available from the authors)

H'Doubler, M. (1966). *Dance: A creative art experience.* Madison, WI: University of Wisconsin Press.

H'Doubler, M. (1978). Paper presented at the AAHPER Gulick Award ceremony. In A. Little (Ed.), *Encores for dance* (pp. 14-17). Washington, DC: American Alliance for Health, Physical Education and Recreation.

Hall, E.T. (1963). A system for the notation of proxemic behavior. *American Anthropologist,* **65,** 1003-1026.

Hall, E.T. (1977). *Beyond culture.* Garden City, NY: Anchor Books.

Halstead, C. (1980). An analysis of attitudes and definitions by selected teachers and pupils toward dance in general and dance in the classroom (Doctoral dissertation, Wayne State University, Detroit, MI). *Dissertation Abstracts International,* **41A,** 4330.

Hankin, T. (1986, November/December). The technique class: How can we help students to dance? *Journal of Physical Education, Recreation and Dance,* **57**(9), 36-37.

Harmon, P., & King, D. (1985). *Expert systems: Artificial intelligence in business.* New York: John Wiley & Sons.

Harnischfeger, A., & Wiley, D.E. (1976). *BTES: Beginning teacher evaluation study.* San Francisco: Far West Laboratory.

Hayes, E.R. (1964). *An introduction to the teaching of dance.* New York: Ronald Press.

Hyatt, J. (1985). *Finding a balance: An approach to movement education.* Ohio: Ohio Arts Council.

Idaho State Department of Education. (1978). *Dance: A guide for Idaho public schools. Grades K-12.* Boise, Idaho: Idaho State Department of Education, Division of Instructional Improvement.

Jacob, E. (1981). *Dancing: A guide for the dancer you can be.* New York: Addison-Wesley.

James, W. (1983). Learning as acting. In F. Burkhardt and R. Bowers (Eds.), *Talks to teachers on psychology: And to students on some of life's ideals.* Cambridge, MA: Harvard University Press.

Jeffries, C.W. (1979). Differential effects of a comparative advance organizer on performance, attitudes, and practice in learning a dance skill (Doctoral dissertation, University of North Carolina, Chapel Hill). *Dissertation Abstracts International,* **41A,** 155.

Jones, N.G.B., & Woodson, R.H. (1979). Describing behavior: The ethnologist's perspective. In M. Lamb, S.J. Suomi, & G.L. Stephenson (Eds.), *Social interactive analysis: Methodological issues* (pp. 97-112). Madison, WI: University of Wisconsin Press.

Joyce, M. (1973). *First steps in teaching creative dance.* Palo Alto, CA: Mayfield.

Joyce, M. (1984). *Dance technique for children.* Palo Alto, CA: Mayfield.

Kruger, M. (1983). *Artificial reality.* Menlo Park, CA: Addison-Wesley.

Lakoff, G., & Johnson, M. (1980). *Metaphors we live by*. Chicago: University of Chicago Press.

Lauffenburger, S.K. (1987). Bartenieff fundamentals: Early detection of potential dance injury. *Journal of Physical Education, Recreation and Dance*, **58**(5), 59-60.

Lessard, E.C. (1980). *Biomechanical analysis of the classical grand plié and two stylistic variations*. Unpublished doctoral dissertation, Texas Women's University, Denton, TX.

Little, A. (1978). The meaning of dance for young children. In A. Little (Ed.), *Encores for dance* (pp. 38-41). Washington, DC: American Association for Health, Physical Education, Recreation and Dance.

Lord, M. (1981-1982). A characterization of dance teacher behaviors in technique and choreography classes. *Dance Research Journal*, **14**(1 & 2), 15-24.

Lunt, J. (1974). A procedure for systematically describing teacher-student verbal and non-verbal interaction in the teaching of choreography (Doctoral dissertation, University of North Carolina, Greensboro). *Dissertation Abstracts International*, **35A**, 2123.

Marr, M. (1975, September). Where do they go when the dancing stops? *Dance Magazine*, p. 64.

McGeoch, J.A., & Irion, A.L. (1952). *The psychology of human learning*. New York: Longman, Green & Co.

McLuen, M. (1964). *Understanding media: The extension of man*. New York: McGraw-Hill.

Mettler, B. (1979). *Materials of dance as a creative art activity*. Tucson, AZ: Mettler Studios.

Mettler, B. (1980). *The nature of dance as a creative art activity*. Tucson, AZ: Mettler Studios.

Metzler, M. (1981). Adapting the academic learning time instructional model to physical education teaching. *Journal of Teaching in Physical Education* **1**(2), 44-55.

Minton, S. (1987). Dance dynamics: Avoiding dance injuries. *Journal of Physical Education, Recreation and Dance*, **58**(5), 29-60.

Minton, S.C. (1981). The effects of several types of teaching cues on postural alignment of beginning modern dancers: A cinematographic analysis (Doctoral dissertation, Texas Women's University). *Dissertation Abstracts International*, **43A**, 1080.

Mitzel, H.E. (1960). Teacher effectiveness. In C.W. Harris (Ed.), *Encyclopedia of educational research* (3rd edition). New York: Macmillan.

Montgomery County Public Schools. (1979). *Program of studies, aesthetic education: Dance, drama/theater, interrelated arts*. Rockville, MD: Maryland Department of Instructional Planning and Development.

Moore, C.L. (1985, April). *Body metaphors and dance instruction*. Paper presented at the annual conference of the American Association for Health, Physical Education, Recreation and Dance, Cincinnati, OH.

Moses, N.H. (1980). The effects of movement notation on the performance, cognition and attitudes of beginning ballet students at the college level (Doctoral dissertation, Boston University). *Dissertation Abstracts International*, **41**, 3479.

New Zealand Department of Education. (1977). *Movement and dance activities*. Wellington, New Zealand: Author.

Oshuns, M.G. (1977). An exploratory study of creative movement as a means of increasing positive self-concept, personal, and social adjustment of selected seventh grade students (Doctoral dissertation, Ohio State University, Columbus). *Dissertation Abstracts International*, **38A**, 555.

Pappalardo, M.D. (1980). The effects of discotheque dancing on selected physiological and psychological parameters of college students (Doctoral dissertation, Boston University. *Dissertation Abstracts International*, **46**, 6192.

Performing together: The arts in education. (1985). Washington, DC: John F. Kennedy Center for the Performing Arts, the Alliance for Arts Education, and the American Association of School Administrators.

Petty, D. (1985). *Torso: An independent research project*. Unpublished manuscript, University of California, Los Angeles, CA.

Pope E., & Gray, J.A. (1983). Cover design. *Journal of Physical Education, Recreation and Dance*, **54**(9), 1.

Pournelle, J. (1986, September 15). Schools fail to educate: Micros fill the gap. *Infoworld*, p. 23.

Raleigh, L. (1986). Interactive compact discs: The next step in CD technology. *Classroom Computer Learning*, **7**(1), 46-47.

Rosenblum, L.A. (1979). Monkeys in time and space. In M.E. Lamb, S.J. Suomi, & G.R. Stephenson (Eds.), *Social interaction analysis* (pp. 269-290). Madison, WI: University of Wisconsin Press.

Rowe, P. (1985). *DANSRESORCE: IBM PC Dancelink Electronic Service*. Unpublished manuscript, New York University, NY.

Ruyter, N. (1986). *Bibliography of dance studies: A database for dance research*. Unpublished manuscript, University of California, Los Angeles, CA.

Sanders, D.H. (1985). *Computers today*. New York: McGraw-Hill.

Schurr, E. (1980). Movement experiences for children: A humanistic approach to elementary school physical education. Englewood Cliffs, NJ: Prentice Hall.

Sealy, D. (1982). Notate: Computerized programs for Labanotation. *Journal for the Anthropological Study of Human Movement*, **1**(2), 70-74.

Sealy, D. (1983). Computer programs for dance notation. *Journal of Physical Education, Recreation and Dance*, **54**(9), 36-37.

Shea, M. (1981). *A kinaesthetic and descriptive study of major body part rotation in the performance of the fouette saute*. Unpublished master's thesis, University of Wisconsin, Madison, WI.

Shuker, V. (1985). *Florida's Dance Certification Task Force proposal*. Unpublished manuscript, Board of Directors, Florida Association for Health, Physical Education, Recreation and Dance.

Simon, A., & Boyer, E.G. (Eds.) (1974). *Mirrors for behavior III: An anthology of observation instruments*. Wyncote, PA: Communication Materials Center.

Simon, H. (1957). Spurious correlations: A causal interpretation. *Models of man*. New York: Wiley.

Singh, B., Beatty, J.C., Booth, K.S., & Ryman, R. (1983). A graphics editor for Benesh movement notation. *Computer Graphics, **17***(3), 51-54.

Stephenson, G.R. (1979). PLEXYN: A computer-compatible grammar for coding complex social interactions. In M.E. Lamb, S. J. Suomi, & G.R. Stephenson (Eds.), *Social interaction analysis* (pp. 157-184). Madison, WI: University of Wisconsin Press.

Stephenson, G.R., & Roberts, T.W. (1977). The SSR System-7: A general encoding system with computerized transcription. *Behavior Research Methods and Instrumentation, **9***(5), 434-441.

Stephenson, G.R., Smith, D.P.R., & Roberts, T. W. (1975). The SSR System: An open format event recording system with computerized transcription. *Behavior Research Methods and Instrumentation, **8***, 259-277.

Stinson, S. (1985). Research as art: New directions for dance educators. In *Dance: The New Zealand experience* (pp. 217-238). Auckland, New Zealand: Auckland Teachers College.

Tannenbaum, E. (1984, August). [Video digitizer demonstration]. Demonstration at Toronto Science Exhibition, Toronto, Canada.

Toffler, A. (1974). The psychology of the future. In A. Toffler (Ed.), *Learning for tomorrow: The role of the future in education* (pp. 3-18). New York: Random House.

Toffler, A. (1981). *The third wave*. New York: Pan Books.

Toffler, A. (1984). *Previews and premises*. Bungay, Suffolk: Chaucer Press.

Trexler, A., & Thornton, R.K. (1986). *The use of a motion detector in dance instruction and performance*. Paper presented at the Arts and Technology Symposium, Connecticut College, New London, CT.

Weber, L., & Smoliar, S.W. (1978). An architecture for the simulation of human movement. *Proceedings of the ACM National Conference, **2***, 737-745.

Weller, R.H. (1971). *Verbal communication in instructional supervision*. New York: Teachers College Press.

Wisconsin Department of Public Instruction. (1981). *Dance: Creative/rhythmic movement education: A conceptual approach for K-12 curriculum development*. Madison, WI: Author.

Witkin, K. (1977). *To move, to learn*. New York: Schocken Books.

Wylie, M., & MacGregor, F.C. (1951). *Growth and culture*. New York: Putnam's Sons.

Index

Numbers in italics indicate that entry is listed in the "Key Terms" section at the end of a chapter.

(Cont.)

(Cont.)

(Cont.)